GRILLING

Good Housekeeping

GRILLING

MOUTHWATERING RECIPES FOR UNBEATABLE BARBECUE

★ GOOD FOOD GUARANTEED ★

HEARST BOOKS
New York

HEARST BOOKS
New York

An Imprint of Sterling Publishing
387 Park Avenue South
New York, NY 10016

ISBN 978-1-61837-155-3

GOOD HOUSEKEEPING

Jane Francisco
EDITOR IN CHIEF
Susan Westmoreland
FOOD DIRECTOR
Sharon Franke
FOOD APPLIANCES AND TECHNOLOGY DIRECTOR

Cover Design: Chris Thompson and Yeon Kim
Interior Design: Yeon Kim
Project Editor: Andrea Lynn

The Good Housekeeping Cookbook Seal guarantees that the recipes in this cookbook meet the strict standards of the Good Housekeeping Research Institute. The Institute has been a source of reliable information and a consumer advocate since 1900, and established its seal of approval in 1909. Every recipe has been triple-tested for ease, reliability, and great taste.

For information about custom editions, special sales, and premium and corporate purchases, please contact Sterling Special Sales at 800-805-5489 or specialsales@sterlingpublishing.com.

Distributed in Canada by Sterling Publishing
^{c}/o Canadian Manda Group, 165 Dufferin Street
Toronto, Ontario, Canada M6K 3H6
Distributed in Australia by Capricorn Link (Australia) Pty. Ltd.
P.O. Box 704, Windsor, NSW 2756, Australia

Manufactured in China

2 4 6 8 10 9 7 5 3 1

www.sterlingpublishing.com

CONTENTS

Jambalaya Sausage Kabobs
(page 60)

Foreword

Simple preparations, enticing aromas, luscious food: Let's talk grilling. It's so easy and the results so satisfying that grilling has become a go-to cooking method. And, with the help of stovetop grill pans, delectable grilled food is a year-round option.

In *Grilling* we've offered our favorite triple-tested recipes for juicy steaks and burgers, fresh vegetables, chicken, seafood, and even pizza. Recipes start with crowd-pleasing appetizers (from bruschette to skewers to wings) and share-worthy salads (including a grilled Chicken Caesar). But the meat of this cookbook is the entrées: Some, like Garden-Fresh Chicken Parmesan and Grilled Halibut with Fresh Dill, are ideal for easy weeknight suppers. Others, like Barbecue Chicken for a Crowd and Baby-Back Ribs Supreme are best for a leisurely weekend barbecue. And, of course, burgers: From chicken and turkey to beef and even a black-bean burger, we have you covered!

These days, vegetables are stars on the grill. Whether you want to grill a platter of mixed veggies or pop on a packet of potatoes, we provide recipes for lots of tempting sides. Our grilled pesto and mozzarella pizzas, veggie burritos, and eggplant parmesan will appeal to vegetarians and the rest of the crew, too, so be sure to make plenty. The book closes with a chapter on sauces, salsa, and rubs that will add mouthwatering flavor to any meat or vegetable.

Before you light your grill (or heat your grill pan), check out "The Way to Great Grilling" on page 8. Our advice will help you get the most out of your grill, whether you favor gas, charcoal, or an electric grill, which allows you to cook without an open flame on a small deck or patio. Grill-pan tips and recipe variations throughout the book provide insight.

From our test kitchen to your backyard, happy grilling!

SUSAN WESTMORELAND
Food Director, *Good Housekeeping*

The Way to Great Grilling

Whether you cook over a shoebox-size hibachi or a state-of-the-art gas grill, you know that the intense heat and savory smoke of grilling impart an incomparable flavor that no other cooking method can. The pleasure of cooking (and eating) outdoors enhances the mealtime experience and, some say, improves the flavors of any dish.

TYPES OF GRILLS

Manufacturers now offer an enticing array of options in grills.

GAS GRILLS have become America's favorite type of grill. And what's not to like? Open the gas valve, turn on the controls, preheat for about ten minutes, and you're ready to go. With gas grills— fueled by either liquid propane or natural gas— you've got a world of features to choose from, including a wide range of BTUs up to almost 50,000; extra burners and warming racks; stainless-steel, cast-iron, or porcelain-coated cooking racks; and stainless-steel or porcelain-coated flavor bars (V-shaped bars that catch dripping fat and return it to the food in the form of tasty smoke).

CHARCOAL GRILLS are fueled by charcoal briquettes or natural hardwood charcoal chunks. They are typically less expensive than their gas-powered brethren. Look for one made of heavy-gauge steel; a porcelain-enamel coating will give you better protection from rust. If you're cooking for one or two, consider the hibachi, a small cast-iron grill that's just right for a pocket-sized patio.

ELECTRIC GRILLS offer an alternative to messing around with propane tanks or charcoal. Plug it in, and you're ready to go. Or, if you live where char-coal or gas are not allowed on the terrace, patio, or deck, there are tabletop versions as well as full-size electric grills available; just be sure to position your grill within reach of a grounded outlet.

GRILLING EQUIPMENT

Here are the basics, plus some extras.

GRILL TOPPER If you often grill delicate foods such as seafood and vegetables, you'll want a grill topper, a perforated metal sheet or tray that provides a nearly smooth surface for grilling. It allows you to virtually "stir-fry" cut-up foods over the flames.

GRILLING BASKET Another good option for delicate or small foods like kabobs, vegetables, shrimp, or fish fillets. Once the food is inside and the basket is clamped shut, you can toss and turn the entire thing at once—easy!

TONGS Better than a fork for turning foods because tongs don't pierce the surface and release juices.

SPATULA Use a long-handled spatula with a heatproof handle for flipping burgers and moving food around on the grill topper.

SKEWERS Long metal skewers are a must for kabobs. Choose skewers with flat shafts rather than round ones; this will prevent food from slipping or turning as it cooks.

BASTING BRUSH A heatproof handle and long shaft are essentials. Choose (nearly indestructible) nonstick silicone bristles over natural or synthetic.

THERMOMETERS There are two types. The first measures the internal temperature of the food; choose from an instant-read thermometer, which is inserted into the center of the food when it's nearly finished, or a thermometer that consists of a probe with digital readout, which you insert into the food as it goes onto the grill. The second type is a grill surface thermometer, which measures the heat of the fire; it's especially useful when you're cooking large items "low" and "slow" and need to maintain an even temperature for many hours.

GRILLING MITTS Make sure they're long to protect more of your forearm and well insulated to protect you from intense heat. Heavy suede mitts are excellent.

METAL-BRISTLED SCRUB BRUSH Use this to clean the grill rack. The best time for this? While the grill is still hot.

For the Fire

Gas and electric grills are easy to light; just follow the manufacturer's directions. For a charcoal grill, to make sure you have enough briquettes, spread an even layer over the bottom of the firebox. And be sure to leave enough time after starting the fire for the coals to develop a light layer of ash—about twenty minutes. Here are options to help you get the fire going.

CHIMNEY STARTER This is an open-ended metal cylinder with a handle. Stuff crumpled newspaper in the bottom of it, fill the top portion with briquettes, then light the paper through an opening in the bottom. The briquettes will burn to ash-covered readiness, at which point you can carefully dump them out into the firebox.

ELECTRIC STARTER A loop-shaped heating element with a handle. Place it in a bed of briquettes, plug it in, and the briquettes will ignite.

LIQUID FIRE STARTER Saturate briquettes with the liquid, then wait for a minute before lighting. By the time the coals are ready for proper cooking, the fluid will have burned off and will not affect the flavor of the food. Never add liquid starter to a fire that's already burning or to hot coals; a spark could ignite the whole can.

SOLID FIRE STARTER Place these waxy-looking cubes in the firebox, pile briquettes on top, and light. They're safer to handle and less aromatic than liquid starter.

SELF-STARTING BRIQUETTES These are impregnated with starter fluid. A match will ignite them immediately. Don't add them to a fire that's already lit.

Choose Your Cooking Method

One key to successful grilling is cooking over the right kind of heat—direct or indirect—at the right level for the food you're preparing.

DIRECT COOKING The gas grill is preheated with all the burners on or, in a charcoal grill, the prepared coals are spread evenly. Food is placed on the grill rack directly over the heat source. This method works best with foods that take less than twenty-five minutes, such as steaks, chops, and vegetables. Direct heat is necessary for searing, which gives meats that nice crusty surface.

INDIRECT COOKING Place your food on the grill rack of a gas grill, over the drip pan. Preheat the burners on the two outer sides for a three-burner grill (or on one side for a two-burner grill). Set the food over the unheated burner. For a charcoal grill, push the briquettes to the edges of the firebox and place a drip pan in the middle before placing your food on the rack. Indirect cooking is best for longer-cooking meats such as roasts and whole chickens or turkeys that might be scorched or dried out by direct heat. Consider placing the food in a pan or grilling basket (see page 8) rather than directly on the grill rack.

TO COVER OR NOT TO COVER? Most grill manufacturers—of both gas and charcoal grills—recommend closing the cover for all grilling. Covering the grill reduces flare-ups, helps prevent charring, and greatly shortens cooking time.

MAINTAINING PROPER HEAT For long, slow cooking, you may need to adjust the controls on your gas grill. It's a bit trickier with a charcoal model. If the fire is too hot, close or partially close vents (top, bottom, or both); if it's not hot enough, open the vents fully or add more briquettes after each additional hour as the manufacturer recommends. Most gas and some charcoal grills have thermometers to monitor the interior temperature without lifting the lid (uncovering causes the temperature to drop quickly).

TO TEST THE HEAT OF A CHARCOAL GRILL Hold your palm above the coals at cooking height (about 6 inches from coals or 2 inches above the rack): If you can keep your palm in position for just 2 to 3 seconds, the fire is hot (above 375°F); 4 to 5 seconds, the fire is medium (above 350°F); 5 to 6 seconds, the fire is low (above 200°F).

Recipes by Icon

We've included icons throughout to make it easy to search for recipes by category, including 30 minutes or less, low calorie, heart healthy, and make ahead dishes.

⊘ 30 MINUTES OR LESS

These easy weekday meals and treats are perfect for busy home cooks. Each require 30 minutes or less to prepare—from kitchen to table!

♥ HEART HEALTHY

If you're looking for heart-healthy options, here's great choices for every meal. Each main dish contains 5 grams or less saturated fat, 150 milligrams or less cholesterol, and 480 milligrams or less sodium. Each appetizer or side dish contains 2 grams or less saturated fat, 50 milligrams or less cholesterol, and 360 milligrams or less sodium.

☺ LOW CALORIE

These recipes will come in handy if you're keeping track of your daily caloric intake. Main-dish meals (which include a starch or fruit) that are 450 calories or less per serving are included, along with all other main dishes that are 300 calories or less per serving. Sides and desserts that are 150 calories or less per serving are also labeled.

▭ MAKE AHEAD

For convenience, you can make all (or a portion) of these recipes ahead of time. The individual recipes indicate which steps you can complete ahead of time, or indicate how long you can refrigerate or freeze the completed dish.

Grilling Times

Here are USDA temperature guidelines for grilled foods. Temperatures should be taken in the thickest part of food; the thermometer should not touch bone, fat, or gristle. (Note: Temperatures for beef are for medium doneness). Let all meat rest 3 minutes before carving or serving.

CUT OF MEAT	COOK TO INTERNAL TEMPERATURE	APPROXIMATE COOKING TIME
Steaks (porterhouse, T-bone, sirloin, rib-eye, top round):		
3/4-inch thick	145ºF	6–8 minutes
1-inch thick	145ºF	11–14 minutes
Steaks (flank or skirt)	145ºF	15–20 minutes
Beef tenderloin, whole	145ºF	30–40 minutes
All burgers (beef, pork, lamb, poultry; 1-inch thick)	160ºF	10–12 minutes
Pork chops (rib or loin; 1-inch thick)	145ºF	12–14 minutes
Pork tenderloin, whole	145ºF	15–25 minutes
Pork tenderloin steaks	145ºF	6 minutes
Chicken legs, bone-in	165ºF	35–40 minutes
Chicken thighs, bone-in	165ºF	12–15 minutes
Chicken thighs, boneless	165ºF	10–12 minutes
Chicken breasts, bone-in	165ºF	30–35 minutes
Chicken breasts, boneless	165ºF	10–12 minutes
Whole chicken (3 pounds)	165ºF	1 hour 15 minutes

Shrimp with Asian Barbecue Sauce (page 14)

1

Starters & Salads

The grill isn't just good for entrees but also lends itself to refreshing salads and made-in-a-snap appetizers. There's grilled bread slices topped with a mixture of chopped tomatoes and ricotta salata, grilled wings tossed in a spicy hot pepper sauce, or wedges of fire-smoked green-onion pancakes. Hearty salads include a twist on the original Caesar topped with chicken and a Thai-style salad topped with thinly sliced grilled steak strips that can stand-in for a main course. Seafood offerings include shrimp that are skewered and glossed with an Asian-style barbecue sauce or garlic-tossed clams and mussels. Whether feeding a crowd for a get-together or for the start of a meal, these grilling delights will please everyone.

|KEY TO ICONS|

☻ 30 MINUTES OR LESS   ♥ HEART HEALTHY   ☺ LOW CALORIE   🛒 MAKE AHEAD

Shrimp WITH
ASIAN BARBECUE SAUCE

Char-grilled shrimp skewers are made even more delicious when you dip them into this delectable hoisin-based sauce seasoned with fresh ginger and five-spice powder. For photo, see page 12.

PREP: 15 MINUTES   **GRILL:** 3 TO 4 MINUTES   **MAKES:** 8 APPETIZER SERVINGS

Romaine lettuce leaves

1¼ pounds large shrimp, shelled and deveined, with tail part of shell left on if you like

8   (10- to 12-inch) wooden or metal skewers

⅓   cup hoisin sauce

3   tablespoons ketchup

1½ teaspoons grated, peeled fresh ginger

¼   teaspoon Chinese five-spice powder

2   tablespoons rice vinegar

2   tablespoons water

1 Lightly grease grill rack. Prepare outdoor grill for direct grilling over medium heat.

2 Arrange lettuce on platter and set aside. Thread shrimp on skewers.

3 In small bowl, stir hoisin sauce, ketchup, ginger, five-spice powder, and 1 tablespoon vinegar to make Asian Barbecue Sauce. Remove ¼ cup barbecue sauce to ramekin; stir in water and remaining 1 tablespoon vinegar and reserve to use as dipping sauce.

4 Brush shrimp with some barbecue sauce from bowl. Place shrimp on hot grill rack over medium heat and cook 2 minutes. Brush with some sauce; turn, brush with remaining sauce, and grill until shrimp turn opaque throughout, 1 to 2 minutes longer.

5 Serve shrimp on skewers over romaine with reserved dipping sauce.

....

EACH SERVING: ABOUT 95 CALORIES, 12G PROTEIN, 7G CARBOHYDRATE, 2G TOTAL FAT (0G SATURATED), 88MG CHOLESTEROL, 270MG SODIUM ♥ ☺

GARLICKY GRILLED
Clams and Mussels

Buy your shellfish from a store with high turnover, and plan to serve the day of purchase. If you're not cooking shellfish right away, refrigerate in a large bowl covered with a couple of layers of wet paper towels, not on ice, until the grill is hot.

PREP: 20 MINUTES   **GRILL:** 8 TO 10 MINUTES   **MAKES:** 8 APPETIZER SERVINGS

4   tablespoons butter or trans fat-free margarine, cut into pieces

2   tablespoons olive oil

3   garlic cloves, minced

1   large shallot, minced (¼ cup)

½   cup dry white wine

¼   teaspoon crushed red pepper

2   pounds mussels, scrubbed, with beards removed

2   dozen littleneck clams, scrubbed

⅔   cup loosely packed fresh parsley leaves, coarsely chopped

lemon and/or lime wedges

French bread slices

1   Prepare outdoor grill for covered direct grilling over medium-high heat.

2   Place butter and oil in large disposable foil roasting pan (about 16" by 12½"). Place pan on hot grill rack over medium-high heat and heat until butter has melted. Remove pan from grill. Add garlic, shallot, wine, and crushed red pepper; stir to combine. Add mussels and clams, spreading out to an even layer. Cover pan tightly with foil.

3   Return pan to grill rack. Cover grill and cook until mussels and clams open, 8 to 10 minutes.

4   Discard any mussels or clams that have not opened. Sprinkle with parsley and serve with lemon and/or lime wedges and French bread.

....

EACH SERVING: ABOUT 180 CALORIES, 14G PROTEIN, 5G CARBOHYDRATE, 11G TOTAL FAT (7G SATURATED), 65MG CHOLESTEROL, 135MG SODIUM

TOMATO AND RICOTTA
Salata Bruschetta

Slabs of rustic bread, grilled, rubbed with garlic and drizzled with olive oil: Bruschetta, Italy's beloved and easy appetizer. It's often topped with savory ingredients, here we use ripe tomatoes and ricotta salata, a lightly salted and pressed sheep's milk cheese. Ricotta salata can be found at Italian markets and specialty food stores.

PREP: 15 MINUTES   **GRILL:** 6 TO 10 MINUTES   **MAKES:** 16 BRUSCHETTA

1   pound (about 5 medium) ripe plum tomatoes, seeded and cut into ½-inch pieces

4   ounces ricotta salata or feta cheese, cut into ¼-inch pieces

2   tablespoons extra-virgin olive oil

1   tablespoon finely chopped red onion

1   tablespoon chopped fresh basil

2   teaspoons balsamic vinegar

¼   teaspoon salt

¼   teaspoon coarsely ground black pepper

8   slices country-style bread (each about 4" by 3" by ½" thick)

1   garlic clove, cut in half

1 Prepare outdoor grill for direct grilling over medium heat, or lightly spray large ridged grill pan with nonstick cooking spray, then heat over medium until hot.

2 In medium bowl, gently toss tomatoes with ricotta salata, oil, onion, basil, vinegar, salt, and pepper. If not serving right away, cover tomato mixture and let stand at room temperature for up to 2 hours.

3 Place bread slices on hot grill rack or pan over medium heat and grill until lightly toasted, 3 to 5 minutes on each side. Rub 1 side of each toast slice with cut side of garlic and cut the toast in half. Discard garlic.

4 Just before serving, spoon tomato mixture over garlic-rubbed side of toast slices.

EACH BRUSCHETTA: ABOUT 80 CALORIES, 2G PROTEIN 9G CARBOHYDRATE, 4G TOTAL FAT (1G SATURATED), 6MG CHOLESTEROL, 236MG SODIUM ♥ ♥ ▣

TUSCAN WHITE-BEAN BRUSCHETTA

Prepare toast as directed for Tomato and Ricotta Salata Bruschetta but prepare topping as follows: In bowl, with fork, lightly mash **1 can (15 ½ to 19 ounces) white kidney beans (cannellini)**, rinsed and drained, with 1 tablespoon fresh lemon juice. Stir in **1 tablespoon olive oil, 2 teaspoons chopped fresh parsley, 1 teaspoon minced fresh sage, ¼ teaspoon salt, and ⅛ teaspoon coarsely ground black pepper.** Just before serving, spoon mixture over garlic-rubbed side of toast slices. Sprinkle with **1 teaspoon chopped fresh parsley.** Makes 16 bruschetta.

....

EACH BRUSCHETTA: ABOUT 35 CALORIES, 2G PROTEIN, 4G CARBOHYDRATE, 1G TOTAL FAT (0G SATURATED), 0MG CHOLESTEROL, 77MG SODIUM 💚 ❤️ 🍱

FIRED-UP GREEN-ONION **Pancakes**

These tempting appetizers are cooked right on the grill for a rustic look and great flavor. If you like, the dough can be prepared through step 4 up to twenty-four hours ahead, covered loosely with greased plastic wrap, and refrigerated. When you're ready, proceed as directed.

PREP: 20 MINUTES PLUS DOUGH RISING   **GRILL:** 4 TO 6 MINUTES PER BATCH
MAKES: 18 APPETIZER SERVINGS

1¼ cups warm water (105° to 115°F)

1   package active dry yeast

1   teaspoon sugar

about 4¼ cups all-purpose flour

1¼ cups chopped green onions (about 12)

1   tablespoon olive oil

1   tablespoon Asian sesame oil

2   teaspoons salt

1   teaspoon ground black pepper

soy sauce or plum sauce for dipping

1 In small bowl, combine warm water, yeast, and sugar; stir to dissolve. Let stand 5 minutes, or until foamy.

2 In large bowl, combine 1½ cups flour, green onions, olive oil, sesame oil, salt, pepper, and yeast mixture. Stir until blended. Gradually stir in 2½ cups flour. With floured hand, knead mixture in bowl until combined.

3 Turn dough onto lightly floured surface and knead 10 minutes, until smooth and elastic, working in more flour (about ¼ cup) if necessary.
4 Shape dough into ball; place in greased large bowl, turning dough to grease top. Cover bowl with plastic wrap and let stand in warm place (80° to 85°F) until doubled in volume, about 1 hour.
5 Prepare outdoor grill for direct grilling over medium heat.
6 Punch down dough. Turn onto lightly floured surface; cover and let rest 15 minutes.
7 Shape dough into 6 balls. Firmly press each ball into an 8-inch round. Place 3 rounds on hot grill rack and grill until grill marks appear on underside and dough stiffens, 2 to 3 minutes. With tongs, turn rounds over and grill until grill marks appear on underside and pancakes are cooked through, 2 to 3 minutes longer. Repeat with remaining dough. Cut each pancake into 6 wedges; serve with soy sauce or plum sauce on the side.

EACH SERVING: ABOUT 130 CALORIES, 4G PROTEIN, 25G CARBOHYDRATE, 2G TOTAL FAT (0G SATURATED), 1G FIBER, 0MG CHOLESTEROL, 240MG SODIUM ♥ ☺ 🧺

GRILLED **Buffalo Wings**

Here's a crowd-pleaser. We made the tangy blue-cheese dipping sauce with reduced-fat mayonnaise, cutting calories but not the great taste.

PREP: 20 MINUTES   **GRILL:** 25 TO 27 MINUTES   **MAKES:** 8 APPETIZER SERVINGS

BLUE-CHEESE DIPPING SAUCE

- 1 container (8 ounces) sour cream (about ¾ cup)
- 4 ounces blue cheese, crumbled (about 1 cup)
- ¾ cup reduced-fat mayonnaise
- 1 green onion, finely chopped
- 2 tablespoons cider vinegar
- 1 teaspoon Worcestershire sauce
- ¼ teaspoon salt

BUFFALO WINGS

- 4 pounds medium chicken wings (about 24)
- ¾ cup hot pepper sauce (see tip)
- celery and carrot sticks

1 Prepare Blue-Cheese Dipping Sauce: In small bowl, with wire whisk, mix sour cream, blue cheese, mayonnaise, green onion, vinegar, Worcestershire sauce, and salt until well combined. Cover and refrigerate until ready to use or up to 3 days. Makes about 2 cups.

2 Prepare outdoor grill for covered direct grilling over medium heat.

3 Meanwhile, Prepare Buffalo Wings: Separate wings at joints; refrigerate tips for another use. Place wings on hot grill rack. Cover grill and cook wings, turning occasionally, until browned, about 20 minutes. Brush wings generously with some hot pepper sauce and grill, brushing with remaining sauce and turning frequently, until glazed and juices run clear when thickest part of wing is pierced with tip of knife, 5 to 7 minutes longer.

4 Serve wings with dipping sauce, celery, and carrot sticks.

EACH SERVING WINGS: ABOUT 300 CALORIES, 27G PROTEIN, 1G CARBOHYDRATE 20G TOTAL FAT (6G SATURATED), 86MG CHOLESTEROL, 675MG SODIUM

EACH TABLESPOON SAUCE: ABOUT 45 CALORIES, 1G PROTEIN, 1G CARBOHYDRATE 4G TOTAL FAT (2G SATURATED), 8MG CHOLESTEROL, 105MG SODIUM 🗑

TIP

Hot pepper sauce is a milder variety of hot pepper sauce that adds tang and flavor, not just heat. It can be found in the condiment section, near the ketchup, in the supermarket.

PANZANELLA SALAD WITH
Grilled Chicken

Show off the fresh flavors of tomato and basil with this effortless salad.

2 tablespoons red wine vinegar

1 garlic clove, crushed with garlic press

3/4 teaspoon salt

1/2 teaspoon freshly ground black pepper

4 tablespoons olive oil

4 ounces country-style bread (1/4 small loaf), cut into 3/4-inch-thick slices

2 medium red peppers, each cut lengthwise into quarters

1 medium red onion, cut into 1/2-inch-thick slices

1 pound skinless, boneless chicken breast-halves

2 pounds plum tomatoes (12 medium), cut into 1-inch chunks

1/4 cup loosely packed small fresh basil leaves or 2 tablespoons chopped leaves

1 Prepare outdoor grill for covered direct grilling over medium heat.

2 Meanwhile, in large bowl, whisk together vinegar, garlic, 1/2 teaspoon salt, 1/4 teaspoon pepper, and 2 tablespoons olive oil until blended; set aside.

3 In jelly-roll pan, brush bread slices, red peppers, and onion slices with remaining 2 tablespoons olive oil to lightly coat both sides; sprinkle with remaining 1/4 teaspoon salt and pepper. With tongs, place bread slices, red peppers, onion slices, and chicken on hot grill rack over medium heat.

4 Cover grill and cook bread about 3 minutes or until lightly toasted, turning once. Cook peppers and onion about 8 minutes or until lightly browned and tender, turning once. Cook chicken about 12 minutes or until chicken loses its pink color throughout, turning once. As bread, vegetables, and chicken are done, transfer to cutting board. Cut bread slices, chicken, peppers, and onions into 1/2-inch pieces.

5 Into vinaigrette in bowl, stir tomatoes, basil, bread, peppers, onions, and chicken; toss to combine. Scoop into bowls to serve.

EACH SERVING: ABOUT 405 CALORIES, 32G PROTEIN, 33G CARBOHYDRATE, 17G TOTAL FAT (3G SATURATED), 6G FIBER, 66MG CHOLESTEROL, 690MG SODIUM

PORTOBELLO AND
Prosciutto Salad

Thick and meaty portobello mushrooms have a natural affinity for the grill. Save the stems, which are woody, and use in soups or stocks, where they'll lend an earthy flavor.

PREP: 30 MINUTES **GRILL:** ABOUT 9 MINUTES **MAKES:** 4 APPETIZER SERVINGS

2 bunches arugula (about 8 ounces total), trimmed

2 tablespoons balsamic vinegar

2 tablespoons olive oil

2 tablespoons minced shallots

2 tablespoons chopped fresh parsley

1/4 teaspoon salt

1/4 teaspoon coarsely ground black pepper

4 portobello mushrooms (about 1½ pounds total), stems removed

8 ounces thinly sliced prosciutto

1/2 cup Parmesan cheese curls shaved with vegetable peeler (1 ounce)

1 Prepare outdoor grill for direct grilling over medium heat. Arrange arugula on platter.

2 In small bowl, with wire whisk, mix vinegar, oil, shallots, parsley, salt, and pepper until blended.

3 Place mushrooms, stem side down, on hot grill rack over medium heat. Brush mushrooms with 1 tablespoon dressing. Grill 4 minutes. Turn mushrooms and brush with 2 tablespoons dressing. Grill until tender, about 5 minutes longer.

4 Thinly slice mushrooms and arrange on arugula. Spoon remaining dressing over salad. Arrange prosciutto on platter with salad. Top with Parmesan curls.

EACH SERVING: ABOUT 270 CALORIES, 23G PROTEIN, 9G CARBOHYDRATE, 17G TOTAL FAT (4G SATURATED), 51MG CHOLESTEROL, 1,320MG SODIUM

GRILLED CHICKEN **Caesar Salad**

This classic restaurant-style salad is enhanced with tangy Dijon mustard and homemade crusty croutons.

PREP: 25 MINUTES **GRILL:** 12 TO 15 MINUTES **MAKES:** 4 MAIN-DISH SERVINGS

1 lemon

1 small garlic clove, crushed with garlic press

1 teaspoon Worcestershire sauce

1 teaspoon Dijon mustard

½ teaspoon anchovy paste

3 tablespoons plus 1 teaspoon olive oil

1 teaspoon salt

½ teaspoon coarsely ground black pepper

4 medium skinless, boneless chicken breast halves (about 1¼ pounds)

½ loaf French bread (4 ounces), cut lengthwise in half

1 large head romaine lettuce (about 1¼ pounds), torn into bite-size pieces

¼ cup freshly grated Parmesan cheese

1 Prepare outdoor grill for direct grilling over medium heat.

2 From lemon, grate 2 teaspoons peel and squeeze 2 tablespoons juice.

3 In small bowl, with wire whisk, mix garlic, Worcestershire, mustard, anchovy paste, lemon juice, 3 tablespoons oil, ½ teaspoon salt, and ¼ teaspoon pepper; set aside.

4 Rub chicken with lemon peel and remaining 1 teaspoon oil; sprinkle with remaining ½ teaspoon salt and ¼ teaspoon pepper. Place chicken and bread, cut side down, on hot grill rack over medium heat. Toast bread, turning once, until golden, about 5 minutes. Grill chicken, turning once, until juices run clear when thickest part of breast is pierced with tip of knife, 12 to 15 minutes. Transfer bread and chicken to cutting board. Cut chicken into ½-inch-thick slices. Cut bread into 1-inch cubes to make croutons.

5 To serve, in large bowl, toss chicken with 1 tablespoon dressing. Add lettuce, Parmesan, croutons, and remaining dressing; toss until well coated.

EACH SERVING: ABOUT 405 CALORIES, 40G PROTEIN, 20G CARBOHYDRATE, 18G TOTAL FAT (4G SATURATED), 95MG CHOLESTEROL, 995MG SODIUM ☺

Grilled Shrimp
CORN, AND TOMATO SALAD

Summer goes south of the border in this flavorful salad. Grilling the veggies adds smoky richness.

2   to 3 limes

4   tablespoons olive oil

3/4 teaspoon salt

2   pinches ground red cayenne pepper

1   teaspoon ground coriander

1/2 teaspoon ground cumin

3   ears corn, husks and silks removed

4   ripe medium tomatoes (6 to 8 ounces each), each cut in half and seeded

1   pound large shrimp, shelled and deveined, with tail part of shell left on if you like

2   medium poblano chiles (about 4 ounces each)

1   head green or red leaf lettuce, thinly sliced

1 Prepare outdoor grill for covered direct grilling over medium heat.

2 Meanwhile, from limes, grate 1 teaspoon peel and squeeze 3 tablespoons juice. In cup, with fork, mix lime juice with 2 tablespoons oil, 1/2 teaspoon salt, 1/2 teaspoon lime peel, and pinch cayenne pepper. Set dressing aside.

3 In medium bowl, with fork, mix coriander and cumin with remaining 2 tablespoons oil, 1/2 teaspoon lime peel, 1/4 teaspoon salt, and pinch cayenne pepper. Brush corn and tomatoes with half of oil mixture. Toss shrimp in oil mixture remaining in bowl.

4 Place corn and whole poblanos on hot grill rack over medium heat. Cover grill and cook until corn is browned in spots and skin on poblanos is charred and blistered on all sides, 10 to 12 minutes, turning occasionally. Transfer corn to cutting board. Transfer poblanos to large sheet of foil. Wrap foil around poblanos and allow to steam at room temperature until cool enough to handle, about 15 minutes.

5 Meanwhile, place shrimp and tomatoes on hot grill rack (or hot, flat grill topper). Cover grill and cook shrimp just until opaque throughout, 4 to 5 minutes, turning once. Cook tomatoes until lightly browned, 4 to 6 minutes, turning once. Transfer shrimp to large bowl and tomatoes to cutting board.

6 Remove poblanos from foil. Peel off skins and discard. Cut each poblano lengthwise in half; remove seeds and membranes. Cut poblanos crosswise into thin strips; add to shrimp in bowl. Cut corn kernels from cobs; add to same bowl. Peel off and discard skin from tomatoes. Cut tomatoes into thin strips; add to same bowl. Add 2 tablespoons dressing to shrimp mixture; toss to coat.

7 In another large bowl, toss lettuce with remaining dressing.

8 To serve, place lettuce on platter; top with shrimp mixture.

....

EACH SERVING: ABOUT 340 CALORIES, 25G PROTEIN, 28G CARBOHYDRATE, 16G TOTAL FAT (2G SATURATED), 180MG CHOLESTEROL, 675MG SODIUM ☺

THAI BEEF Salad

Crisp and refreshing—a *perfect* choice for a hot evening.

PREP: 20 MINUTES PLUS MARINATING   **GRILL:** 10 TO 15 MINUTES   **MAKES:** 4 MAIN-DISH SERVINGS

2   tablespoons Asian fish sauce (see tip, page 86)

2½ teaspoons sugar

1   beef top round steak, ¾-inch thick (about 1 pound)

2   to 3 limes

3   tablespoons vegetable oil

¼   teaspoon crushed red pepper

¼   teaspoon coarsely ground black pepper

2   bunches watercress (4 ounces each), tough stems trimmed

1   cup loosely packed fresh mint leaves

1   cup loosely packed fresh cilantro leaves

1   bunch radishes, each cut in half and thinly sliced

½   small red onion, thinly sliced

1 In 8-inch or 9-inch square baking dish, stir 1 tablespoon fish sauce and 1 teaspoon sugar. Add steak, turning to coat; marinate 15 minutes at room temperature or 1 hour in refrigerator, turning occasionally.

2 Prepare outdoor grill for covered direct grilling over medium heat.

3 Meanwhile, from limes, with vegetable peeler, remove peel in 2" by ¾" strips. With sharp knife, cut enough peel crosswise into matchstick-thin strips to equal 1 tablespoon. From limes, squeeze 3 tablespoons juice. In small bowl, whisk lime juice, oil, crushed red pepper, black pepper, and remaining 1 tablespoon fish sauce and 1½ teaspoons sugar until blended.

4 In large bowl, toss watercress, mint, cilantro, radishes, onion, and lime peel; cover and refrigerate until ready to serve.

5 Place steak on hot grill rack over medium heat. Cover grill and cook steak 10 to 15 minutes for medium-rare or until desired doneness, turning once. Transfer steak to cutting board; let stand 10 minutes to allow juices to set for easier slicing. Thinly slice steak on the diagonal across the grain.

6 Add steak and dressing to watercress mixture and toss until well coated. Serve on dinner plates.

....

EACH SERVING: ABOUT 310 CALORIES, 28G PROTEIN, 7G CARBOHYDRATE, 23G TOTAL FAT (4G SATURATED), 73MG CHOLESTEROL, 295MG SODIUM ♥ ☺

Basic Chicken Burgers
(page 42)

2 Chicken & Turkey

Grilling was made for poultry—it renders the skin golden and the delicate meat absorbs the smoke-kissed flavor. Whether it's for chicken breasts wrapped in prosciutto and sage Saltimbocca-style or chicken cutlets topped with layers of mozzarella, tomato slices and basil leaves in a fresh, calorie-lightened take on Chicken Parmesan, it's a no-brainer for weeknight dinners.

For a cookout or outdoor event, turn to Barbecue Chicken for a Crowd, featuring baked chicken pieces on the grill for quick-cooking and basted with homemade barbecue sauce or a whole chicken made fragrant with thyme, lemon and garlic.

Barbecue Chicken FOR A CROWD

To help you enjoy more time with your guests, completely precook the chicken in the oven and keep refrigerated up to a day. When you're ready to dine, all you have to do is warm up the chicken on the grill and brush on our delicious barbecue sauce.

PREP: 30 MINUTES **BAKE/GRILL:** 1 HOUR 20 MINUTES **MAKES:** 10 MAIN-DISH SERVINGS

10 pounds bone-in chicken parts, skin removed, if you like

1 tablespoon olive oil

1 jumbo onion (1 pound), chopped

1 tablespoon grated, peeled fresh ginger

3 garlic cloves, crushed with garlic press

1/4 cup chili powder

1 can (28 ounces) whole tomatoes in puree

1/2 cup cider vinegar

1/4 cup packed dark brown sugar

1/4 cup light (mild) molasses

3 tablespoons Dijon mustard

2 tablespoons Worcestershire sauce

1 teaspoon salt

1 Preheat oven to 425°F. Place chicken pieces in large roasting pan (17" by 11½"); cover tightly with foil. Bake until juices run clear when thickest part of chicken is pierced with tip of knife, about 1 hour. Transfer chicken to large platter; cover and refrigerate until ready to grill.

2 Meanwhile, in 5- to 6-quart saucepot, heat oil over medium heat until hot. (Do not use smaller pan; sauce bubbles up and splatters during cooking—the deeper the pan, the better.) Add onion and ginger; cook, stirring occasionally,

until onion is tender and golden, about 10 minutes. Add garlic and chili powder; cook, stirring, 1 minute longer. Remove saucepot from heat; stir in tomatoes with their puree, vinegar, brown sugar, molasses, mustard, Worcestershire, and salt.

3 Spoon about one-third of sauce into blender. At low speed, puree sauce until smooth; pour sauce into bowl. Repeat with remaining sauce. Return sauce to saucepot; heat to boiling over high heat. Reduce heat to medium and cook, partially covered, 1 minute, stirring occasionally. Cover and refrigerate sauce if not using right away. Sauce will keep up to 1 week in refrigerator or up to 2 months in freezer. Makes about 4½ cups.

4 Prepare outdoor grill for direct grilling over medium heat.

5 Place chicken on hot grill rack and grill, turning once, 10 minutes. Brush barbecue sauce over chicken and grill, turning chicken pieces and brushing with barbecue sauce, until sauce is hot and bubbly and chicken is heated through, about 10 minutes longer.

EACH SERVING WITHOUT SKIN: ABOUT 360 CALORIES, 41G PROTEIN, 21G CARBOHYDRATE 13G TOTAL FAT (3G SATURATED), 121MG CHOLESTEROL, 645MG SODIUM

Grilled Whole Chicken
WITH LEMON AND GARLIC

Use a covered grill to cook this deliciously seasoned chicken. If you're using a charcoal grill, you will need to add ten fresh charcoal briquettes per side to maintain the heat if more than one hour of cooking is required.

PREP: 15 MINUTES   **GRILL:** ABOUT 1 HOUR 15 MINUTES   **MAKES:** 4 MAIN-DISH SERVINGS

1   chicken (about 3-pounds)

1   lemon

1   small bunch fresh thyme

6   garlic cloves, peeled

½   teaspoon salt

¼   teaspoon coarsely ground black pepper

1 Prepare charcoal grill for covered indirect grilling with drip pan as manufacturer directs or preheat gas grill for covered indirect grilling over medium heat.

2 Remove giblets and neck from chicken; refrigerate for another use. Rinse chicken inside and out with cold running water; drain well and pat dry with paper towels.

3 From lemon, grate 2 teaspoons peel. Cut lemon into quarters and set aside. Chop enough thyme leaves to equal 1 teaspoon; reserve remaining sprigs. Into cup, crush 2 garlic cloves with garlic press; reserve remaining 4 cloves. To garlic in cup, add lemon peel, chopped thyme, salt, and pepper; set aside. Place lemon quarters, whole garlic cloves, and 3 thyme sprigs inside cavity of chicken. Reserve remaining thyme sprigs for garnish, if you like.

4 With chicken breast side up, lift wings up toward neck, then fold wing tips under back of chicken so they stay in place. With string, loosely tie legs together. Rub lemon mixture all over outside of chicken.

5 Place chicken on hot grill rack over drip pan or away from heat source on gas grill. Cover grill; cook chicken until juices run clear when thickest part of chicken is pierced with tip of knife, about 1 hour 15 minutes.

6 Place chicken on platter; let stand 10 minutes to allow juices to set for easier carving. Cut into 8 serving pieces and garnish with thyme sprigs, if using. Remove skin from chicken before eating, if you like.

EACH SERVING WITHOUT SKIN: ABOUT 235 CALORIES, 36G PROTEIN, 1G CARBOHYDRATE 9G TOTAL FAT (3G SATURATED), 109MG CHOLESTEROL, 395MG SODIUM ♥ ☺

FLAME-COOKED
Chicken Saltimbocca

So simple, yet so flavorful, this dish will quickly become a part of your outdoor repertoire. Remember, cutlets are thin, so make sure you don't overcook them. These would be delicious served between two layers of grilled focaccia.

PREP: 15 MINUTES   **GRILL:** ABOUT 8 MINUTES   **MAKES:** 8 MAIN-DISH SERVINGS

2   tablespoons fresh lemon juice

1   tablespoon olive oil

8   chicken cutlets or skinless, boneless chicken breast halves with tenderloins removed (2 pounds total)

24 large fresh sage leaves

8   thin slices prosciutto (4 ounces; see tip)

1 Prepare outdoor grill for direct grilling over medium heat.

2 In large bowl, with fork, mix lemon juice and oil. Add chicken and toss to coat.

3 Place 3 sage leaves on each cutlet or breast half, then wrap each with 1 slice prosciutto. Place chicken on hot grill rack over medium heat and grill until juices run clear when thickest part of breast is pierced with tip of knife, about 8 minutes, turning once.

....

EACH SERVING: ABOUT 195 CALORIES, 31G PROTEIN, 1G CARBOHYDRATE, 7G TOTAL FAT (2G SATURATED), 83MG CHOLESTEROL, 410MG SODIUM ♥ ♥ ☺

TIP
If you like, substitute slices of smoked turkey, ham, or Canadian bacon.

Hoisin Chicken WITH
PLUMS AND GREEN ONIONS

This Asian-inspired dish pairs deliciously with sweet plums
and the bite of grilled onions.

PREP: 20 MINUTES PLUS MARINATING   **GRILL:** 34 TO 48 MINUTES   **MAKES:** 4 MAIN-DISH SERVINGS

¼   cup rice vinegar

1   tablespoon Asian sesame oil

1   tablespoon grated, peeled fresh ginger

1   teaspoon Chinese five-spice powder

¼   teaspoon ground red pepper (cayenne)

1   chicken (about 4 pounds), cut into 8 serving pieces, skin removed if you like

2   bunches green onions

1   tablespoon olive oil

¼   teaspoon salt

⅛   teaspoon coarsely ground black pepper

⅓   cup hoisin sauce

1   tablespoon low-sodium soy sauce

4   plums, pitted and halved

1   teaspoon sesame seeds

1 In large bowl, stir vinegar, sesame oil, ginger, five-spice powder, and ground red pepper. Add chicken to bowl and toss to coat. Marinate 15 minutes.

2 Meanwhile, prepare outdoor grill for covered direct grilling over medium heat.

3 Brush green onions with olive oil and sprinkle with salt and black pepper. In small bowl, mix hoisin sauce and soy sauce.

4 Remove chicken from marinade; discard marinade. Grill and cook chicken until juices run clear when thickest part of chicken is pierced with knife, 20 to 25 minutes, turning pieces once. Reserve ¼ cup hoisin mixture for serving; brush chicken with remaining mixture for last minute of cooking. Transfer chicken to platter. Cover; keep warm.

5 Grill onions until lightly charred and tender, 3 to 5 minutes, turning once. Grill plums until lightly charred and softened, 6 to 8 minutes, turning once. Transfer onions and plums to platter with chicken.

6 To serve, sprinkle chicken with sesame seeds. Pass a bowl with reserved hoisin mixture.

EACH SERVING WITHOUT SKIN: ABOUT 465 CALORIES, 48G PROTEIN, 25G CARBOHYDRATE, 19G TOTAL FAT (4G SATURATED), 138MG CHOLESTEROL, 770MG SODIUM

Coffee-Spice Chicken
WITH FRUIT-BASIL SALSA

A jerk-style seasoning of Jamaican allspice and java gives this Caribbean chicken its caffeinated kick. Balancing the heat: a cooling summer salsa of just-picked nectarines and juicy watermelon.

PREP: 30 MINUTES   **GRILL:** 8 TO 10 MINUTES   **MAKES:** 8 MAIN-DISH SERVINGS

3   cups seedless watermelon cubes, cut into ½-inch chunks (from 4-pound piece of watermelon)

1   large ripe nectarine, pitted and cut into ½-inch chunks

3   tablespoons finely chopped red onion

1   tablespoon fresh lemon juice

2   tablespoons instant coffee

1   tablespoon grated, peeled fresh ginger

1   tablespoon olive oil

1¼ teaspoons ground allspice

¾   teaspoon salt

8   skinless, boneless chicken breast-halves (about 3 pounds)

½   cup packed fresh basil leaves, coarsely chopped

1 In medium bowl, combine watermelon, nectarine, onion, and lemon juice. Cover and refrigerate while preparing chicken. Makes 4 cups.

2 Prepare outdoor grill for covered direct grilling over medium heat, or lightly spray large ridged grill pan with nonstick cooking spray, then heat over medium heat until hot.

3 In large bowl, with spoon or fingers, press coffee to pulverize. Add ginger, oil, allspice, and ½ teaspoon salt; stir to combine. Add chicken and toss to evenly coat with spice mixture (you may need to pat spice mixture onto chicken with fingers).

4 Place chicken breasts on hot grill rack or pan over medium heat. Cover and cook 8 to 10 minutes or until juices run clear when thickest part of chicken is pierced with tip of knife, turning once. Transfer chicken to cutting board and let rest 5 minutes. Meanwhile, stir basil and remaining ¼ teaspoon salt into salsa. Slice chicken crosswise and serve with salsa.

EACH SERVING: ABOUT 235 CALORIES, 40G PROTEIN, 8G CARBOHYDRATE, 4G TOTAL FAT (1G SATURATED), 1G FIBER, 99MG CHOLESTEROL, 310MG SODIUM ♥ ☺

GARDEN-FRESH
Chicken Parmesan

This grilled version of an old favorite still has a layer of mozzarella cheese and a sprinkling of Parmesan, but we've replaced the usual tomato sauce with juicy slices of tomato and fresh basil leaves.

PREP: 10 MINUTES   **GRILL:** 8 TO 10 MINUTES   **MAKES:** 4 MAIN-DISH SERVINGS

- 4 medium skinless, boneless chicken breast halves (about 1¼ pounds total)
- 2 teaspoons olive oil
- ½ teaspoon salt
- ¼ teaspoon coursely ground black pepper
- 4 ounces part-skim mozzarella cheese, cut into ¼-inch-thick slices, each slice cut crosswise in half
- 2 ripe medium tomatoes (6 to 8 ounces each), cut into ¼-inch-thick slices
- ¼ cup freshly grated Parmesan cheese
- ¾ cup loosely packed fresh basil leaves

1 Prepare outdoor grill for direct grilling over medium-high heat.

2 If necessary, pound chicken breasts to uniform ¼-inch thickness. Coat chicken with oil and sprinkle with salt and pepper.

3 Place chicken on hot grill rack and grill 4 minutes. Turn chicken and top with mozzarella, tomatoes, and Parmesan. Cook until juices run clear when chicken is pierced with tip of knife, 4 to 6 minutes longer.

4 Transfer chicken to platter and top with basil leaves.

EACH SERVING: ABOUT 340 CALORIES, 49G PROTEIN, 4G CARBOHYDRATE, 13G TOTAL FAT (5G SATURATED), 129MG CHOLESTEROL, 615MG SODIUM

APRICOT-GINGER **Chicken Legs**

Double this quickly-put-together sauce and set aside half to serve for dipping. If the sauce is too thick to spread, combine all the ingredients in a small saucepan and heat at the edge of the grill until the sauce is a spreading consistency. For a change of pace, substitute orange marmalade for the apricot preserves.

PREP: 10 MINUTES   **GRILL:** 35 MINUTES   **MAKES:** 6 MAIN-DISH SERVINGS

- 2 green onions, chopped
- ½ cup apricot preserves
- ⅓ cup ketchup
- 2 tablespoons cider vinegar
- 1 tablespoon plus 1 teaspoon grated, peeled fresh ginger
- 1 tablespoon plus 1 teaspoon soy sauce
- 6 large chicken legs (about 3¾ pounds)

1 Prepare outdoor grill for direct grilling over medium heat.

2 In small bowl, mix green onions, apricot preserves, ketchup, vinegar, ginger, and soy sauce.

3 Place chicken legs on hot grill rack over medium heat and grill until golden on both sides, about 10 minutes. Then, to avoid charring, stand chicken legs upright, leaning one against the other. Rearrange pieces from time to time and grill, brushing chicken legs frequently with apricot mixture during last 10 minutes of grilling, until fork-tender and juices run clear when pierced with knife, about 25 minutes longer.

EACH SERVING: ABOUT 410 CALORIES, 37G PROTEIN, 22G CARBOHYDRATE, 19G TOTAL FAT (5G SATURATED), 129MG CHOLESTEROL, 520MG SODIUM

TIP

If you prefer a smooth sauce, start with ¾ cup of apricot preserves and push it through a fine-mesh sieve to remove large chunks.

Mojito-Rubbed Chicken
WITH GRILLED PINEAPPLE

Bring a taste of the tropics to your barbecue with this refreshing mint-lime combo. To round out your meal, serve with steamed broccolini spears.

PREP: 20 MINUTES   GRILL: 10 MINUTES   MAKES: 4 MAIN-DISH SERVINGS

4   medium skinless, boneless chicken breast halves (about 1½ pounds)

2   limes

1   tablespoon olive oil

1   medium pineapple (3½ pounds), peeled and cut into ½-inch-thick slices

¼   cup loosely packed fresh mint leaves, chopped

½   teaspoon salt

¼   teaspoon ground black pepper

1 Prepare outdoor grill for direct grilling over medium heat, or heat large ridged grill pan over medium until hot.

2 Meanwhile, place chicken breast-halves between 2 sheets of plastic wrap; with meat mallet, pound to an even ½-inch thickness.

3 From 1 lime, grate 1 teaspoon peel and squeeze 2 tablespoons juice. Cut remaining lime into wedges; set aside. In small bowl, combine oil, lime peel, and juice. Lightly brush pineapple on both sides with lime mixture; set aside remaining lime mixture in bowl. Place pineapple slices on hot grill rack and cook 10 minutes or until browned on both sides, turning once.

4 Stir mint into remaining lime mixture and pat onto both sides of chicken. Sprinkle chicken with salt and pepper to season both sides. Place chicken on hot grill rack or pan over medium heat; cook 5 minutes or until chicken is browned on both sides and no longer pink throughout, turning once. Serve chicken with pineapple and lime wedges.

EACH SERVING: ABOUT 320 CALORIES, 40G PROTEIN, 27G CARBOHYDRATE, 6G TOTAL FAT (1G SATURATED), 3G FIBER, 99MG CHOLESTEROL, 385MG SODIUM ♥ ♥ ☺

JAMAICAN JERK **Chicken Kabobs**

Originally, jerk seasoning was used to season pork shoulder, which was "jerked" apart into shreds before serving. Nowadays, this popular power-packed seasoning is found on everything from fish to tofu.

PREP: 15 MINUTES PLUS MARINATING **GRILL:** ABOUT 10 MINUTESS **MAKES:** 4 MAIN-DISH SERVINGS

2 green onions, chopped

1 jalapeño chile, seeded and minced

1 tablespoon minced, peeled fresh ginger

2 tablespoons white wine vinegar

2 tablespoons Worcestershire sauce

3 teaspoons vegetable oil

1 teaspoon ground allspice

1 teaspoon dried thyme

½ teaspoon plus ⅛ teaspoon salt

1 pound skinless, boneless chicken breast-halves, cut into 12 pieces

1 red pepper, stem and seeds removed, cut into 1-inch pieces

1 green pepper, stem and seeds removed, cut into 1-inch pieces

4 (10-inch) metal skewers

1 In blender or in food processor with knife blade attached, process green onions, jalapeño, ginger, vinegar, Worcestershire, 2 teaspoons oil, allspice, thyme, and ½ teaspoon salt until paste forms.

2 Place chicken in small bowl or ziptight plastic bag and add green-onion mixture, turning to coat chicken. Cover bowl or seal bag and refrigerate 1 hour to marinate.

3 Meanwhile, in small bowl, toss red and green peppers with remaining 1 teaspoon oil and remaining ⅛ teaspoon salt.

4 Prepare outdoor grill for direct grilling over medium heat, or lightly spray large ridged grill pan with cooking spray, then heat over medium until hot. Alternately thread chicken and pepper pieces on each skewer.

5 Place kabobs on hot grill rack or pan over medium heat. Brush kabobs with any remaining marinade. Cook kabobs 5 minutes; turn and cook until chicken loses its pink color throughout, about 5 minutes longer.

....

EACH SERVING: ABOUT 180 CALORIES, 27G PROTEIN, 6G CARBOHYDRATE, 5G TOTAL FAT (1G SATURATED), 66MG CHOLESTEROL, 525MG SODIUM ☺

BASIC **Chicken Burgers**

If you're looking for a straightforward burger, here it is. We also have suggestions for jazzing it up to please a variety of cravings, so pick your favorite flavor: teriyaki, barbecue, or herb. For photo, see page 28.

PREP: 20 MINUTES   **GRILL:** ABOUT 12 MINUTES   **MAKES:** 4 MAIN-DISH SERVINGS

1   pound ground chicken breast

1   medium carrot, peeled and grated (½ cup)

2   green onions, minced

1   garlic clove, crushed with garlic press

4   hamburger buns, split and toasted

sliced cucumber, lettuce leaves, and green onions (optional)

1 Prepare outdoor grill for direct grilling over medium heat, or lightly spray large ridged grill pan with nonstick cooking spray, then heat over medium until hot.

2 Prepare burgers: In medium bowl, combine ground chicken, carrot, green onions, and garlic.

3 On waxed paper, shape chicken mixture into four 3½-inch round patties (mixture will be very soft and moist).

4 Place patties on hot grill rack or pan over medium heat and grill, turning once, until juices run clear when center of burger is pierced with tip of knife, about 12 minutes. (An instant-read meat thermometer inserted horizontally into center should register 170°F.) If you have a grill with widely spaced grates, you may want to place burgers on a perforated grill topper to keep them intact.

5 Place burgers on toasted buns. Serve with cucumber slices, lettuce leaves, and green onions, if you like.

EACH BURGER: ABOUT 275 CALORIES, 30G PROTEIN, 24G CARBOHYDRATE, 5G TOTAL FAT (1G SATURATED), 72MG CHOLESTEROL, 310MG SODIUM ♥ ☺

TERIYAKI CHICKEN BURGERS

Prepare Basic Burgers as directed, but add **2 tablespoons soy sauce, 1 tablespoon seasoned rice vinegar, 2 teaspoons grated, peeled fresh ginger,** and **2 teaspoons Asian sesame oil** to ground chicken mixture in step 2. (Prepare burger mixture just before cooking to prevent ginger from changing texture of meat.)

EACH TERIYAKI CHICKEN BURGER: ABOUT 305 CALORIES, 31G PROTEIN, 26G CARBOHYDRATE, 8G TOTAL FAT (2G SATURATED), 72MG CHOLESTEROL, 940MG SODIUM ☺

BARBECUE CHICKEN BURGERS

Prepare Basic Burgers as directed, but add **2 tablespoons chili sauce, 1 tablespoon light (mild) molasses, 2 teaspoons cayenne pepper sauce, 2 teaspoons Worcestershire sauce,** and **¼ teaspoon salt** to ground chicken mixture in step 2.

EACH BARBECUE CHICKEN BURGER: ABOUT 295 CALORIES, 31G PROTEIN, 30G CARBOHYDRATE, 5G TOTAL FAT (1G SATURATED), 72MG CHOLESTEROL, 715MG SODIUM ☺

HERB CHICKEN BURGERS

Prepare Basic Burgers as directed, but add **2 tablespoons finely chopped fresh dill, 1 tablespoon dried mint, 1 tablespoon fresh lemon juice, 1 teaspoon ground cumin, ½ teaspoon salt,** and **⅛ teaspoon ground red pepper (cayenne)** to ground chicken mixture in step 2.

EACH HERB CHICKEN BURGER: ABOUT 280 CALORIES, 31G PROTEIN, 25G CARBOHYDRATE, 5G TOTAL FAT (1G SATURATED), 72MG CHOLESTEROL, 605MG SODIUM ☺

MEDITERRANEAN
Chicken Sandwiches

You can use this Provençal-style olive mayonnaise as a topping for tomatoes, too. Double the grilled flavor and grill the bread (about 1½ minutes per side) before spreading with the mayonnaise.

PREP: 25 MINUTES **GRILL:** 10 TO 12 MINUTES **MAKES:** 4 MAIN-DISH SERVINGS

1   teaspoon fennel seeds

½   teaspoon dried thyme

½   teaspoon salt

¼   teaspoon coarsely ground black pepper

4   medium skinless, boneless chicken breast-halves (about 1¼ pounds total)

¼   cup Kalamata olives, pitted and minced

2   tablespoons mayonnaise

1   loaf (8 ounces) Italian bread

2   ripe small tomatoes (4 ounces each), each cut into 4 slices

1 Prepare outdoor grill for direct grilling over medium heat.

2 In mortar with pestle, crush fennel seeds with thyme, salt, and pepper. Rub both sides of chicken breasts with fennel-seed mixture; set aside.

3 In small bowl, mix olives and mayonnaise. Cut bread crosswise into 4 equal pieces, then cut each piece horizontally in half. Spread olive mixture evenly on cut sides of bread; set aside.

4 Place chicken on hot grill rack over medium heat and grill until juices run clear when thickest part of breast is pierced with tip of knife, 10 to 12 minutes, turning once. Transfer chicken to cutting board.

5 To assemble sandwiches, cut chicken breasts crosswise into ¼-inch-thick slices. On bottom halves of bread, layer sliced chicken and tomatoes. Replace top halves of bread.

EACH SERVING: ABOUT 400 CALORIES, 38G PROTEIN, 32G CARBOHYDRATE, 12G TOTAL FAT (2G SATURATED), 86MG CHOLESTEROL, 910MG SODIUM ☺

Turkey Burgers
WITH MINTED YOGURT SAUCE

Yogurt, feta, and mint add a taste of Greece to this flavorful but slimmed-down (and heart-healthy) summer favorite.

PREP: 10 MINUTES   **GRILL:** 12 TO 13 MINUTES   **MAKES:** 4 MAIN-DISH SERVINGS

½   cup plus 2 tablespoons plain fat-free Greek yogurt

2   green onions, green and white parts separated and thinly sliced

½   cup packed fresh mint leaves, finely chopped

1   pound lean ground turkey

1½ ounces feta cheese, finely crumbled

1½ teaspoons ground coriander

⅛   teaspoon salt

½   teaspoon coursely ground black pepper

2   whole-wheat pitas, cut in half

2   tomatoes, thinly sliced

1 Prepare outdoor grill for covered direct grilling over medium heat.

2 In small bowl, combine ½ cup yogurt, white parts of green onions, and half of mint; refrigerate.

3 In large bowl, with hands, combine turkey, feta, coriander, salt, pepper, green parts of green onions, remaining mint, and remaining 2 tablespoons yogurt. Mix well, then form into 3½-inch round patties (each ¾-inch thick).

4 Place turkey patties on hot grill rack over medium heat; cover and cook 12 to 13 minutes or just until meat loses its pink color throughout, turning once. (Burgers should reach an internal temperature of 165°F.) During last 2 minutes of cooking, add pitas to grill. Cook 2 minutes or until warmed, turning once.

5 Open pitas. Divide burgers, tomato slices, and yogurt sauce among pitas.

EACH SERVING: ABOUT 310 CALORIES, 30G PROTEIN, 24G CARBOHYDRATE, 12G TOTAL FAT (4G SATURATED), 4G FIBER, 90MG CHOLESTEROL, 460MG SODIUM ♥ ❤ ☺

Turkey Cutlets, INDIAN-STYLE

Delicious with a squeeze of fresh lime or with Peach Salsa or Pineapple-Tomato Salsa (both page 133) served alongside. For a festive presentation, set out bowls of yogurt, store-bought mango chutney, fluffy basmati rice, and chopped fresh cilantro alongside the cutlets.

PREP: 15 MINUTES   **GRILL:** 5 TO 7 MINUTES   **MAKES:** 6 MAIN-DISH SERVINGS

2   large limes

1/3   cup plain low-fat yogurt

1   tablespoon vegetable oil

2   teaspoons minced, peeled fresh ginger

1   teaspoon ground cumin

1   teaspoon ground coriander

1   teaspoon salt

1   garlic clove, crushed with garlic press

6   turkey cutlets (about 1½ pounds total)

1 Prepare outdoor grill for direct grilling over medium heat.

2 From 1 lime, grate 1 teaspoon peel and squeeze 1 tablespoon juice. Cut remaining lime into wedges; reserve.

3 In large bowl, mix lime peel, lime juice, yogurt, oil, ginger, cumin, coriander, salt, and garlic until blended.

4 Just before grilling, add turkey cutlets to bowl with yogurt mixture; stir to coat. (Do not let cutlets marinate in yogurt mixture; their texture will become mealy.)

5 Place cutlets on hot grill rack over medium heat and grill until they just lose their pink color throughout, 5 to 7 minutes. Discard excess marinade. Serve with lime wedges.

EACH SERVING: ABOUT 160 CALORIES, 29G PROTEIN, 3G CARBOHYDRATE, 3G TOTAL FAT (1G SATURATED), 71MG CHOLESTEROL, 450MG SODIUM

SPICED GRILLED **Turkey Breast**

Soaking a whole turkey breast overnight in a spiced salt solution, or brine, produces exceptionally tender and flavorful meat. You can also use this brine for a whole chicken before roasting.

PREP: 35 MINUTES PLUS BRINING AND STANDING
GRILL: 25 TO 30 MINUTES   **MAKES:** 12 MAIN-DISH SERVINGS

SPICED TURKEY BREAST

- ¼ **cup sugar**
- ¼ **cup kosher salt**
- 2 **tablespoons cracked black pepper**
- 2 **tablespoons ground ginger**
- 1 **tablespoon ground cinnamon**
- 1 **whole boneless turkey breast (about 4 pounds), skin removed, breast cut in half**
- 4 **garlic cloves, crushed with side of chef's knife**

CHIPOTLE HONEY MUSTARD GLAZE

- 2 **tablespoons honey**
- 2 **tablespoons Dijon mustard**
- 1 **chipotle chile in adobo, minced**
- 1 **teaspoon balsamic vinegar**

PEACH SALSA (PAGE 113)

1 Prepare Spiced Turkey Breast: In 2-quart saucepan, heat sugar, salt, pepper, ginger, cinnamon, and *1 cup water* to boiling over high heat. Reduce heat to low; simmer 2 minutes. Remove from heat; stir in *3 cups ice water*.

2 Place turkey breast in large ziptight plastic bag; add brine and garlic. Seal bag, pressing out excess air. Place bag in bowl and refrigerate, turning occasionally, 24 hours.

3 Prepare outdoor grill for covered direct grilling over medium heat.

4 Prepare Chipotle Honey Mustard Glaze: In small bowl, stir honey, mustard, chipotle, and vinegar until blended. Set aside.

5 Remove turkey from bag; discard brine and garlic. With paper towels, pat turkey dry and brush off most of pepper. With long-handled basting brush, oil grill rack. Place turkey on hot grill rack over medium heat. Cover grill and cook turkey 20 minutes, turning once. Brush turkey with glaze and cook 5 to 10 minutes longer (depending on thickness of breast), brushing and turning frequently, until temperature on instant-read meat thermometer inserted into thickest part of breast reaches 165°F. (Internal temperature will rise 5°F upon standing.) Place turkey on cutting board and let stand 10 minutes to allow juices to set for easier slicing.

6 While turkey rests, prepare Peach Salsa.

7 Serve turkey hot, or cover and refrigerate to serve cold, with the salsa on the side.

....

EACH SERVING TURKEY: ABOUT 170 CALORIES, 34G PROTEIN, 4G CARBOHYDRATE, 1G TOTAL FAT (0G SATURATED), 94MG CHOLESTEROL, 555MG SODIUM ☺ 🍴

Jerk Steak Kabobs with Pineapple Salsa (page 56)

3 Beef, Pork & Lamb

The sizzle of the grill does the work for you when it comes to juicy meat, charring the exterior golden-brown and sealing in succulence. Spicy Flank Steak with Quesadillas appeal to adults and kids alike with flame-charred corn and Mexican-style cheese encased between tortillas alongside the steak. Other weeknight options fresh from the grill are Soy-Scallion Flank Steak, Jambalaya Sausage Kabobs, or BLT Burgers.

A red-wine and rosemary marinade boosts a porterhouse steak. An elegant meal or dinner party is made easy with Filet Mignon with Horseradish Salsa or an Indian-Spiced Butterflied Lamb. Our triple-tested recipes are guaranteed to please everyone—you for their quick cooking time, and your family for their deliciousness.

KEY TO ICONS

⏱ 30 MINUTES OR LESS ♥ HEART HEALTHY ☺ LOW CALORIE 🍲 MAKE AHEAD

RED-WINE AND ROSEMARY
Porterhouse

This robust marinade can season a thick, juicy steak in fifteen minutes. Marinate for up to one hour for more intense flavor. It's also good on lamb, pork, or poultry. Serve with Lemon-Garlic Potato Packet (page 106) and Crumb-Topped Tomatoes (page 95).

PREP: 10 MINUTES PLUS MARINATING   **GRILL:** 15 TO 20 MINUTES PLUS STANDING   **MAKES:** 4 MAIN-DISH SERVINGS

½   cup dry red wine (see tip)

1   tablespoon Worcestershire sauce

1   tablespoon tomato paste

1   tablespoon Dijon mustard

1   tablespoon balsamic vinegar

1   tablespoon chopped fresh rosemary

1   large garlic clove, crushed with garlic press

1   beef loin porterhouse or T-bone steak, 1½ inches thick (about 1½ pounds)

1   lemon, cut into wedges

1 In small bowl, stir together wine, Worcestershire, tomato paste, mustard, vinegar, rosemary, and garlic.

2 Place steak in large ziptight plastic bag. Pour wine marinade over steak, turning to coat. Seal bag, pressing out excess air. Let stand 15 minutes at room temperature or refrigerate up to 1 hour, turning once.

3 Prepare outdoor grill for direct grilling over medium heat.

4 Remove steak from bag; discard marinade. Place steak on hot grill rack over medium heat and grill, turning once, 15 to 20 minutes for medium-rare or until desired doneness.

5 Transfer steak to cutting board; let stand 10 minutes to allow juices to set for easier slicing. Thinly slice steak and serve with lemon wedges.

EACH SERVING: ABOUT 395 CALORIES, 32G PROTEIN, 1G CARBOHYDRATE, 28G TOTAL FAT (11G SATURATED), 104MG CHOLESTEROL, 125MG SODIUM

TIP

For a dry red wine that would work well in this recipe, try a Shiraz, Merlot, Chianti, or Cabernet.

BARBECUED **Beef Brisket**

Make this rich brisket ahead and then finish on an outdoor grill. Slow-cook the meat on the stovetop up to two days ahead, then glaze with sauce and grill for twenty minutes to heat through. Leftovers, if there are any, can be heated in a little sauce and spooned over crusty rolls.

PREP: 3 HOURS 25 MINUTES   **GRILL:** 20 MINUTES   **MAKES:** 12 MAIN-DISH SERVINGS

1   fresh beef brisket (about 4½ pounds), trimmed

1   medium onion (8 ounces), peeled and cut into quarters

1   large carrot, peeled and cut into 1½-inch pieces

1   bay leaf

1   teaspoon whole black peppercorns

¼   teaspoon whole allspice (see tip)

Chunky Barbecue Sauce (page 118)

1 In 8-quart Dutch oven, place brisket, onion, carrot, bay leaf, peppercorns, and allspice. Add enough *water to cover* and heat to boiling over high heat. Reduce heat to low; cover and simmer until meat is fork-tender, about 3 hours.

2 Meanwhile, prepare Chunky Barbecue Sauce.

3 When brisket is done, transfer to platter. If not serving brisket right away, cover and refrigerate until ready to serve.

4 Prepare outdoor grill for direct grilling over medium heat.

5 Place brisket on hot grill rack over medium heat and grill 10 minutes. Turn brisket over and grill 5 minutes. Spoon 1 cup barbecue sauce on top of brisket and cook until brisket is heated through, about 5 minutes longer. (Do not turn brisket after topping with sauce.) If you like, reheat remaining sauce in small saucepan on grill. Thinly slice brisket across grain and serve with sauce.

....

EACH SERVING WITH SAUCE: ABOUT 500 CALORIES, 30G PROTEIN, 4G CARBOHYDRATE, 40G TOTAL FAT (15G SATURATED), 117MG CHOLESTEROL, 185MG SODIUM 🍲

TIP

Allspice is available in two forms, whole berries or ground. It gets its name from the fact that it tastes like a combination of cloves, cinnamon, and nutmeg.

Filet Mignon WITH
HORSERADISH SALSA

Juicy steaks taste even better with our flavor-packed salsa. Looking for a new vegetable idea? Try grilling young onions right along with the meat.

PREP: 15 MINUTES   **GRILL:** 10 TO 12 MINUTES   **MAKES:** 4 MAIN-DISH SERVINGS

HORSERADISH SALSA

- 3 ripe medium tomatoes (about 1 pound), cut into ½-inch pieces
- 1 cup loosely packed fresh parsley leaves, chopped
- ½ small red onion, minced
- 2 tablespoons bottled white horseradish
- 1 tablespoon balsamic vinegar
- 1 tablespoon olive oil
- ½ teaspoon salt

FILET MIGNON

- 1 teaspoon coarsely ground black pepper
- 1 teaspoon olive oil
- ½ teaspoon salt
- ¼ teaspoon dried thyme
- 1 garlic clove, crushed with garlic press
- 4 beef tenderloin steaks (filet mignon), 1-inch thick (about 6 ounces each)

1 **Prepare Horseradish Salsa:** In medium bowl, combine tomatoes, parsley, onion, horseradish, vinegar, oil, and salt. Refrigerate up to 2 hours.

2 **Prepare Filet Mignon:** Prepare outdoor grill for direct grilling over medium heat, or lightly spray large ridged grill pan with nonstick cooking spray, then heat over medium until hot.

3 In cup, mix pepper, oil, salt, thyme, and garlic. Rub pepper mixture all over steaks.

4 Grill steaks, turning once, 10 to 12 minutes for medium-rare or until desired doneness. Serve steaks with Horseradish Salsa.

EACH SERVING STEAK ONLY: ABOUT 330 CALORIES, 39G PROTEIN, 9G CARBOHYDRATE, 15G TOTAL FAT (4G SATURATED), 89MG CHOLESTEROL, 710MG SODIUM

EACH CUP SALSA: ABOUT 35 CALORIES, 1G PROTEIN, 4G CARBOHYDRATE, 2G TOTAL FAT (0G SATURATED), 0MG CHOLESTEROL, 180MG SODIUM

TIP

This pepper rub also works beautifully with flank steak, skirt steak, or any sirloin cut.

Spicy Flank Steak
WITH QUESADILLAS

If you have the time, let the spice-rubbed steak sit in the fridge up to one hour before grilling for more intense flavor.

PREP: 15 MINUTES **GRILL:** 14 TO 16 MINUTES PLUS STANDING **MAKES:** 4 MAIN-DISH SERVINGS

1   lime

4   teaspoons chili powder

1½ teaspoons ground cumin

1   teaspoon brown sugar

¼   teaspoon salt

1   beef flank steak (about 1¼ pounds), well trimmed

3   ears corn, husks and silks removed

1   large red pepper, stem and seeds removed, cut into quarters

4   (8-inch) flour tortillas

3   ounces reduced-fat (2%) Mexican-style cheese, shredded (¾ cup)

2   green onions, thinly sliced

plain fat-free Greek yogurt or low-fat sour cream (optional)

1 Prepare outdoor grill for covered direct grilling over medium heat.

2 From lime, grate 1 teaspoon peel and squeeze 1 teaspoon juice. In small bowl, combine lime peel and juice, chili powder, cumin, brown sugar, and salt. Rub steak with chili powder mixture to season both sides.

3 Grill steak and vegetables, covered, until corn is browned in spots, pepper is lightly charred and tender (turning vegetables occasionally), and steak is medium-rare or desired doneness (turning steak once), 12 to 15 minutes. As vegetables are done, transfer to cutting board. Transfer steak to another cutting board; let stand 10 minutes to allow juices to set for easier slicing.

4 When vegetables are cool enough to handle, cut corn kernels from cobs and coarsely chop pepper. Place tortillas on work surface. Divide cheese, green onions, corn, and peppers on half of each tortilla. Fold each tortilla over filling to make 4 quesadillas; grill until browned on both sides, about 2 minutes, carefully turning once. Cut each quesadilla in half.

5 Thinly slice steak and serve with quesadillas and yogurt, if using.

EACH SERVING: ABOUT 515 CALORIES, 41G PROTEIN, 46G CARBOHYDRATE, 20G TOTAL FAT (8G SATURATED), 81MG CHOLESTEROL, 745MG SODIUM ♥

Jerk Steak Kabobs
WITH PINEAPPLE SALSA

The hot Caribbean coating on the meat is the perfect foil for our cool tropical salsa. If you like, flame-cook pineapple wedges next to your kabobs instead of making the salsa. For photo, see page 48.

PREP: 30 MINUTES PLUS MARINATING   GRILL: 8 TO 10 MINUTES   MAKES: 4 MAIN-DISH SERVINGS

PINEAPPLE SALSA

- 1   large lime
- 1   ripe pineapple, peeled, cored, and coarsely chopped
- 1   cup loosely packed fresh cilantro leaves, chopped
- 1   jalapeño chile, seeded and minced
- 1   green onion, thinly sliced
- 1   teaspoon sugar
- ¼   teaspoon salt
- ⅛   teaspoon coursely ground black pepper

STEAK KABOBS

- 2   green onions, minced
- 2   tablespoons fresh lime juice
- 2   tablespoons brown sugar
- 1   tablespoon Worcestershire sauce
- 1   tablespoon grated, peeled fresh ginger
- 1   teaspoon vegetable oil
- 1   teaspoon salt
- 1   teaspoon dried thyme
- 1   teaspoon ground allspice
- ½   teaspoon ground red pepper (cayenne)
- 1   boneless beef top sirloin steak, 1¼ inches thick (about 1½ pounds) cut into 1¼-inch cubes
- 4   (12-inch) metal skewers

1 Prepare Pineapple Salsa: From lime, grate ½ teaspoon peel and squeeze 2 tablespoons juice. In medium bowl, mix lime peel and juice with pineapple, cilantro, jalapeño, green onion, sugar, salt, and pepper. Cover and refrigerate up to 4 hours.

2 Prepare Steak Kabobs: Prepare outdoor grill for direct grilling over medium heat, or lightly spray large ridged grill pan with nonstick cooking spray, then heat over medium until hot.

3 Meanwhile, in large bowl, mix green onions, lime juice, brown sugar, Worcestershire, ginger, oil, salt, thyme, allspice, and ground red pepper. Add steak cubes and toss to coat; let stand 15 minutes at room temperature.

4 Thread steak cubes on skewers. Place skewers on hot grill rack or pan over medium heat; cook 8 to 10 minutes for medium-rare or until desired doneness, turning occasionally. Serve kabobs with salsa.

....

EACH SERVING KABOBS ONLY: ABOUT 295 CALORIES, 34G PROTEIN, 10G CARBOHYDRATE 13G TOTAL FAT (5G SATURATED), 102MG CHOLESTEROL, 650MG SODIUM ☺

EACH CUP SALSA: ABOUT 20 CALORIES, 0G PROTEIN, 5G CARBOHYDRATE, 0G TOTAL FAT, 0MG CHOLESTEROL, 35MG SODIUM 🍴

SOY-SCALLION **Flank Steak**

A marinade of Asian ingredients adds zip to grilled steak.

PREP: 15 MINUTES PLUS MARINATING   **GRILL:** 12 TO 14 MINUTES PLUS STANDING   **MAKES:** 8 MAIN-DISH SERVINGS

⅓ cup soy sauce

3 cloves garlic, crushed with garlic press

2 tablespoons grated, peeled fresh ginger

2 tablespoons rice vinegar

1 tablespoon Asian sesame oil

1 tablespoon sugar

½ teaspoon ground red pepper (cayenne)

1 bunch green onions

1 beef flank steak (2½ pounds)

1 In medium bowl, whisk soy sauce, garlic, ginger, vinegar, oil, sugar, and ground red pepper until sugar dissolves. Reserve 2 tablespoons marinade; cover and set aside. Transfer remaining marinade to large ziptight plastic bag.

2 Thinly slice green onions; reserve ¼ cup for garnish. Add steak and remaining green onions to bag, turning to coat. Seal bag, pressing out excess air. Place bag on plate and refrigerate 2 hours or overnight, turning over several times.

3 Prepare outdoor grill for covered direct grilling over medium heat. Remove steak from marinade, scraping off excess solids, and place on hot grill grate.

4 Discard marinade in bag. Cover grill and cook steak 12 to 14 minutes for medium-rare or until desired doneness, turning once. Let steak stand 10 minutes to set juices for easier slicing.

5 In small bowl, combine *2 tablespoons hot water* with reserved marinade; drizzle over steak to serve and sprinkle with reserved green onion.

....

EACH SERVING: ABOUT 260 CALORIES, 34G PROTEIN, 1G CARBOHYDRATE, 12G TOTAL FAT (5G SATURATED), 0G fiber, 60mg cholesterol, 315mg sodium ♥ ☺

Steak Sandwiches
WITH GRILLED ONIONS

Marinating the steak with a sweet and savory blend of flavors and grilling it takes this classic sandwich to a new level.

PREP: 15 MINUTES PLUS MARINATING   **GRILL:** 12 TO 15 MINUTES   **MAKES:** 4 MAIN-DISH SERVINGS

¼ **cup soy sauce**

¼ **cup balsamic vinegar**

1 **tablespoon brown sugar**

1 **tablespoon fresh thyme leaves**

¼ **teaspoon coursely ground black pepper**

1 **beef flank steak (about 1¼ pounds)**

1 **(12-inch) metal skewer**

1 **medium red onion (about 8 ounces), cut into 4 thick slices**

8 **slices sourdough bread, toasted on grill if you like**

2 **ripe medium tomatoes (6 to 8 ounces each), sliced**

1 **bunch (5 ounces) arugula, trimmed**

1 In large ziptight plastic bag, mix soy sauce, vinegar, brown sugar, thyme, and pepper. Add steak, turning to coat. Seal bag, pressing out excess air. Place bag on plate; let marinate 15 minutes at room temperature or 1 hour in the refrigerator, turning several times.

2 Prepare outdoor grill for covered direct grilling over medium heat.

3 Meanwhile, for easier handling, insert skewer horizontally through onion slices; set aside.

4 Remove steak from marinade; pour marinade into 1-quart saucepan. Heat marinade over high heat to boiling; boil 2 minutes.

5 Place steak and onion slices on hot grill rack over medium heat. Cover grill and cook steak and onions, brushing both with marinade occasionally and turning once, until onions are browned and tender and meat is medium-rare, 12 to 15 minutes. Transfer steak to cutting board; let stand 10 minutes to allow juices to set for easier slicing. Separate onion into rings.

6 Thinly slice steak diagonally across grain. Arrange onion rings and steak on 4 slices of bread; spoon any meat juices from board over onion and steak. Top with tomatoes, arugula, and remaining 4 slices of bread.

EACH SERVING: ABOUT 450 CALORIES, 40G PROTEIN, 51G CARBOHYDRATE, 10G TOTAL FAT (4G SATURATED), 84MG CHOLESTEROL, 802MG SODIUM ☺

THE PERFECT **Burger**

A key to a delicious, juicy burger is to handle the ground beef as little as possible. Shape your burgers without compacting them too much.

PREP: 10 MINUTES PLUS MARINATING   **GRILL**: 8 TO 10 MINUTES   **MAKES**: 4 MAIN-DISH SERVINGS

4   (12-inch) bamboo skewers

1¼ pounds ground beef chuck

½   teaspoon coarsely ground black pepper

1   teaspoon salt

1   large sweet onion (12 ounces), cut into ½-inch-thick rounds

4   hamburger buns, split

4   green-leaf lettuce leaves

2   ripe medium tomatoes (6 to 8 ounces each), thinly sliced

1 Soak skewers in water to cover 20 minutes. Meanwhile, prepare outdoor grill for covered direct grilling over medium heat, or preheat large ridged grill pan over medium until very hot.

2 Shape ground beef into 4 patties. Sprinkle pepper and ¾ teaspoon salt on both sides of patties. For easier handling, insert one skewer horizontally through each onion slice. Sprinkle onion with remaining ¼ teaspoon salt.

3 Place burgers and onion on hot grill rack or pan; cook 8 to 10 minutes for medium or to desired doneness, turning once. Onion should be browned and tender. About 1 minute before burgers are done, add buns, cut sides down, to grill. Grill just until toasted.

4 Serve burgers on buns with lettuce, tomato, and onion.

EACH BURGER: ABOUT 485 CALORIES, 31G PROTEIN, 33G CARBOHYDRATE, 25G TOTAL FAT (9G SATURATED), 96MG CHOLESTEROL, 920MG SODIUM

JAMBALAYA SAUSAGE **Kabobs**

Kielbasa is a great choice for a weekday meal on the grill. Already cooked, it just needs a turn over the coals to develop a tasty brown crust. For photo, see page 6.

For photo, see page 6.

PREP: 25 MINUTES   **GRILL:** 10 TO 12 MINUTES   **MAKES:** 4 MAIN-DISH SERVINGS

8 (12-inch) wooden skewers or 4 long metal skewers

2 small zucchini (about 6 ounces each), cut diagonally into ¾-inch-thick slices

1 red pepper, stem and seeds removed, cut into 1¼-inch pieces

½ small Vidalia onion, cut into 4 wedges, keeping wedges intact with toothpicks

1 tablespoon plus 1 teaspoon olive oil

2 teaspoons Cajun seasoning

1 package (16 ounces) light kielbasa or other fully cooked smoked sausage, cut diagonally into 1-inch chunks

1 large stalk celery, chopped

1 package (8.8 ounces) white rice, fully cooked

1 ripe medium tomato (6 to 8 ounces), chopped

2 tablespoons water

1 Prepare outdoor grill for covered direct grilling over medium heat. Meanwhile, if using wooden skewers, soak in water 20 minutes.

2 In large bowl, toss zucchini, red pepper, onion, 1 tablespoon oil, and 1 teaspoon Cajun seasoning. Alternately thread zucchini, red pepper, onion, and kielbasa onto skewers.

3 Place skewers on hot grill rack over medium heat. Cover grill and cook until kielbasa browns and vegetables are tender-crisp, 10 to 12 minutes, turning skewers occasionally. Remove skewers to platter; keep warm.

4 In nonstick 10-inch skillet, heat remaining 1 teaspoon oil over medium heat. Add celery and remaining 1 teaspoon Cajun seasoning. Cook, covered, until celery softens, about 5 minutes, stirring occasionally. Stir in rice, tomato, and water. Cover and cook until rice is hot, about 3 minutes. Serve rice with kabobs.

EACH SERVING WITHOUT RICE: ABOUT 320 CALORIES, 18G PROTEIN, 9G CARBOHYDRATE 26G TOTAL FAT (8G SATURATED), 76MG CHOLESTEROL, 1,160MG SODIUM

EACH SERVING RICE: ABOUT 85 CALORIES, 2G PROTEIN, 17G CARBOHYDRATE, 1G TOTAL FAT (0G SATURATED), 0MG CHOLESTEROL, 150MG SODIUM

BLT BURGERS

Take a classic American sandwich and turn it into a yummy burger.

PREP: 15 MINUTES   **GRILL:** 10 TO 12 MINUTES   **MAKES:** 4 MAIN-DISH SERVINGS

¼ cup ketchup

¼ cup light mayonnaise

1 tablespoon yellow mustard

1¼ pounds ground beef chuck

8 slices bacon

4 sesame-seed buns, split

Sliced sweet onion, sliced tomato, and romaine
   lettuce leaves

1 Prepare outdoor grill for direct grilling over medium heat, or lightly spray large ridged grill pan with nonstick cooking spray, then heat over medium until hot.

2 In small bowl, stir ketchup, mayonnaise, and mustard until blended. Set aside. Makes about ½ cup.

3 Shape ground beef into four ¾-inch-thick burgers. Wrap each burger with 2 strips bacon, perpendicular to each other.

4 Place burgers on hot grill rack or pan over medium heat; cook 10 to 12 minutes for medium or until desired doneness, turning once.

5 During last 2 minutes of cooking burgers, place buns, cut sides down, on grill rack and heat until lightly toasted. Serve burgers on buns with onion, tomato, lettuce, and sauce on the side.

....

EACH BURGER: ABOUT 575 CALORIES, 34G PROTEIN, 27G CARBOHYDRATE, 36G TOTAL FAT (12G SATURATED), 111MG CHOLESTEROL, 870MG SODIUM ✔

Inside-Out Burgers
WITH AVOCADO AND SPROUTS

Creative condiments—guacamole and alfalfa sprouts—and Cheddar in the center give lean beef patties extra zip.

PREP: 15 MINUTES **GRILL:** ABOUT 12 MINUTES **MAKES:** 4 MAIN-DISH SERVINGS

1½ pounds 90% lean ground beef

2 ounces sharp cheddar cheese, shredded (½ cup)

½ teaspoon plus ⅛ teaspoon salt

¼ teaspoon ground black pepper

1 ripe avocado

1 tablespoon fresh lime juice

1 cup alfalfa or radish sprouts

¼ cup loosely packed fresh cilantro leaves, chopped

4 multigrain hamburger buns, split

2 small tomatoes, each cut into 4 wedges

1 Lightly spray large ridged grill pan with nonstick cooking spray, then heat over medium until hot, or prepare outdoor grill for covered direct grilling over medium heat.

2 Meanwhile, on work surface, shape ground beef into eight 3½-inch patties, handling meat as little as possible for best texture. Place Cheddar in center of 4 patties, leaving ½-inch border around each patty's edge. Top with remaining 4 patties; press edges together to seal burgers well. Lightly sprinkle burgers with ½ teaspoon salt and pepper to season both sides.

3 Place burgers on hot grill pan or rack over medium heat, and cook 12 minutes for medium or until desired doneness, turning burgers once halfway through cooking.

4 Meanwhile, in small bowl, mash avocado with lime juice and remaining ⅛ teaspoon salt. In another small bowl, combine alfalfa sprouts and chopped cilantro.

5 Serve burgers on buns with sprout and avocado mixtures. Serve tomato wedges on the side.

EACH BURGER: ABOUT 480 CALORIES, 36G PROTEIN, 25G CARBOHYDRATE, 27G TOTAL FAT (9G SATURATED), 5G FIBER, 102MG CHOLESTEROL, 730MG SODIUM

Fennel-Orange Pork
WITH GRILLED VEGETABLES

Radicchio and Belgian endive, with their
slightly bitter taste, serve as a counterbalance for the pork.

PREP: 15 MINUTES   GRILL: ABOUT 10 MINUTES   MAKES: 4 MAIN-DISH SERVINGS

1   teaspoon fennel seeds

½   teaspoon dried thyme

¼   teaspoon coarsely ground black pepper

¾   teaspoon salt

1   teaspoon freshly grated orange peel

4   pork rib or loin chops, 1 inch thick (about 6 ounces each), trimmed

1   tablespoon olive oil

1   tablespoon balsamic vinegar

2   heads radicchio di Treviso (about 4 ounces each), each cut lengthwise in half, or 1 large round head radicchio (about 8 ounces), cut into 8 wedges

2   large heads Belgian endive (about 5 ounces each), each cut lengthwise into quarters

1 Prepare outdoor grill for direct grilling over medium heat.

2 In mortar with pestle or in ziptight plastic bag with rolling pin, crush fennel seeds with thyme, pepper, and ½ teaspoon salt. Stir orange peel into fennel-seed mixture. With hand, rub both sides of pork chops with fennel-seed mixture.

3 In medium bowl, mix oil, vinegar, and remaining ¼ teaspoon salt. Add radicchio and endive to bowl and gently toss to coat.

4 Place pork chops on hot grill rack over medium heat and grill 5 minutes. Turn chops and add vegetables to grill. Grill until chops have just a hint of pink color in center and vegetables are browned, about 5 minutes longer.

5 Serve pork chops with grilled vegetables.

EACH SERVING: ABOUT 690 CALORIES, 37G PROTEIN, 38G CARBOHYDRATE, 43G TOTAL FAT (16G SATURATED), 172MG CHOLESTEROL, 860MG SODIUM

Pork Loin WITH LEMON, THYME, AND GARLIC

Grill small clusters of grapes for 5 minutes, serve with pork.

PREP: 15 MINUTES   GRILL: ABOUT 50 MINUTES PLUS STANDING   MAKES: 8 MAIN-DISH SERVINGS

4   lemons

4   garlic cloves, crushed with garlic press

2   tablespoons fresh thyme leaves, chopped

1   tablespoon olive oil

½   teaspoon salt

½   teaspoon coarsely ground black pepper

1   boneless pork loin roast (about 3 pounds), trimmed

1 Prepare outdoor grill for covered, indirect grilling over medium heat.

2 From 2 lemons, grate 1 tablespoon peel and squeeze 1 tablespoon juice. Cut each remaining lemon into 4 wedges.

3 In small bowl, combine lemon peel and juice, garlic, thyme, olive oil, salt, and pepper.

4 Make 10 to 12 (1-inch-long and 1½-inch-deep) slits in pork. Rub pork all over with lemon mixture, pushing some into slits.

5 Place pork on hot grill rack and cook over direct heat 10 minutes, turning several times to sear all sides. Move pork to unheated burner or away from the coals; cover and cook until instant-read meat thermometer inserted into center of pork registers 145°F, about 40 minutes. Transfer pork to cutting board; let stand 10 minutes to allow juices to set for easier slicing. (Internal temperature of pork will rise 5°F to 10°F upon standing.)

6 Serve sliced pork with lemon wedges and any juices from cutting board.

....

EACH SERVING: ABOUT 350 CALORIES, 35G PROTEIN, 3G CARBOHYDRATE, 21G TOTAL FAT (7G SATURATED), 112MG CHOLESTEROL, 240MG SODIUM

INDIAN-SPICED **Butterflied Lamb**

For a cool, tangy sauce, a jar of mango chutney, available at the supermarket, can be chopped, mixed with yogurt, and served with the lamb. A crisp green or cucumber salad tossed with chopped fresh cilantro and basmati rice would also be welcome additions to this Indian-style lamb.

PREP: 10 MINUTES PLUS MARINATING   **GRILL:** 20 TO 30 MINUTES   **MAKES:** 10 MAIN-DISH SERVINGS

1   cup plain low-fat yogurt

8   garlic cloves, peeled

1   piece fresh ginger (about 2 inches), peeled and coarsely chopped

1   tablespoon ground coriander

1   tablespoon ground cumin

2   tablespoons fresh lemon juice

2   teaspoons salt

1/4   to 1/2 teaspoon ground red pepper (cayenne)

1   butterflied boneless leg of lamb, trimmed (about 3 pounds; see tip)

1 In blender, puree yogurt, garlic, ginger, coriander, cumin, lemon juice, salt, and ground red pepper until smooth. Pour yogurt mixture into large ziptight plastic bag; add lamb, turning to coat. Seal bag, pressing out excess air. Place bag on plate; refrigerate 1 hour, turning occasionally. (Do not marinate more than 2 hours or texture of meat will change.)

2 Prepare outdoor grill for direct grilling over medium heat.

3 Remove lamb from bag. Pour marinade into small bowl and reserve.

4 Place lamb on hot grill rack over medium heat and grill, turning once, 15 minutes. Brush both sides of lamb with reserved marinade and cook, turning lamb occasionally, 10 to 20 minutes longer for medium-rare or until desired doneness. Thickness of butterflied lamb will vary throughout; cut off sections of lamb as they are cooked and place on cutting board. Let stand 10 minutes to allow juices to set for easier slicing. Thinly slice lamb to serve.

EACH SERVING: ABOUT 280 CALORIES, 27G PROTEIN, 3G CARBOHYDRATE, 17G TOTAL FAT (7G SATURATED), 95MG CHOLESTEROL, 550MG SODIUM ☺

KOREAN-STYLE SESAME **Short Ribs**

Marinating overnight makes these meaty ribs irresistible. Serve with a spicy cabbage slaw or a cool rice salad. If you like, sprinkle the short ribs with sesame seeds and thinly sliced green onion just before serving.

PREP: 15 MINUTES PLUS MARINATING   **GRILL:** 20 TO 25 MINUTES   **MAKES:** 6 MAIN-DISH SERVINGS

4   pounds beef chuck short ribs, cut into 2-inch pieces

½   cup reduced-sodium soy sauce

4   teaspoons minced, peeled fresh ginger

2   teaspoons Asian sesame oil

3   large garlic cloves, minced

1 With sharp knife, cut ¼-inch-deep slashes in meaty side of short ribs at ½-inch intervals.

2 In large ziptight plastic bag, combine soy sauce, ginger, sesame oil, and garlic. Add short ribs, turning to coat. Seal bag, pressing out as much air as possible. Place bag in 13" by 9" baking dish and refrigerate overnight to marinate, turning once.

3 Prepare outdoor grill for direct grilling over medium heat.

4 Lift ribs from bag, reserving marinade. Place ribs on hot grill rack and brush with remaining marinade. Grill, turning ribs occasionally, 20 to 25 minutes for medium-rare or until desired doneness.

EACH SERVING: ABOUT 745 CALORIES, 34G PROTEIN, 3G CARBOHYDRATE, 65G TOTAL FAT (27G SATURATED), 142 MG CHOLESTEROL, 880MG SODIUM 📷

Baby-Back Ribs SUPREME

Only fifteen minutes of grilling time! The trick: Steam the seasoned ribs for an hour in the oven up to two days before barbecuing. With both the ribs and the BBQ sauce prepared in advance, this succulent grill could easily become a part of your summer weeknight repertoire.

PREP: 1 HOUR 15 MINUTES **GRILL:** 15 MINUTES **MAKES:** 8 MAIN-DISH SERVINGS

4 teaspoons grated, peeled fresh ginger

2 teaspoons freshly grated lemon peel

3/4 teaspoon salt

2 garlic cloves, crushed with garlic press

4 racks pork baby-back ribs (about 1 pound each; see tip)

2 cups boiling water

2 cups Secret-Recipe Barbecue Sauce (page 119)

1 Preheat oven to 350°F. In cup, mix ginger, lemon peel, salt, and garlic until combined. Rub ginger mixture on ribs.

2 Place ribs in large roasting pan (15½" by 11½"), overlapping slightly. Pour boiling water into roasting pan. Cover pan tightly with foil and place in oven. Steam ribs 1 hour.

3 Meanwhile, prepare Secret-Recipe Barbecue Sauce.

4 Carefully remove foil from roasting pan (escaping steam is very hot). Remove ribs from pan; discard water. Ribs may be grilled immediately or refrigerated up to 2 days before grilling.

5 Prepare outdoor grill for direct grilling over medium heat.

6 Place ribs, meat side up, on hot grill rack; grill 5 minutes, turning once. Turn ribs over; brush with barbecue sauce and grill 5 minutes. Turn ribs over again; brush with more sauce and grill 5 minutes longer. Cut racks into 2-rib portions; serve with remaining sauce.

EACH SERVING: ABOUT 460 CALORIES, 27G PROTEIN, 12G CARBOHYDRATE, 33G TOTAL FAT (12G SATURATED), 129MG CHOLESTEROL, 570MG SODIUM 🗑

TIP
When buying baby backs, look for ribs that are meaty, with a minimum of visible fat.

Salmon BLTs with Lemon-Dill Mayonnaise (page 79)

4 Fish & Seafood

We'll admit it—fish can be tricky to tackle. Grilling it is one of the easiest ways to deliver flavorful, fuss-free seafood. Pat herbs to salmon and let the grill do its magic as in Provençal Salmon with Tomato-Olive Relish. A simple mustard and lemon mix glazes Scallop and Cherry Tomato Skewers. Use the grill to bring out the best in the myriad offerings from the ocean.

Go the sandwich route with ginger and soy sauce-spiked Asian Tuna Burgers or grilled salmon and bacon in Salmon BLTs with Lemon-Dill Mayonnaise. Other easy dinners include grilled tilapia piled into a tortilla with avocado and fixings for fish tacos, and Thai Snapper in Foil Packets. An edamame salad pairs with Miso-Glazed Salmon and grilled pineapple wedges accompany Jamaican Jerk Catfish. Bursting with rich flavors and smokiness, these recipes bring grill-worthy options to any occasion.

KEY TO ICONS

◐ 30 MINUTES OR LESS   ♥ HEART HEALTHY   ☺ LOW CALORIE   🗐 MAKE AHEAD

Provençal Salmon
WITH TOMATO-OLIVE RELISH

Lightly season thick salmon steaks with Herbes de Provence, a store-bought mix of dried herbs—often a combination of lavender, basil, thyme, and sage—that is classic in the South of France.

PREP: 25 MINUTES   **GRILL:** ABOUT 8 MINUTES   **MAKES:** 4 MAIN-DISH SERVINGS

TOMATO-OLIVE RELISH

- 1 lemon
- ½ cup green olives, pitted and coarsely chopped
- 1 ripe medium tomato (6 to 8 ounces), cut into ¼-inch chunks
- 1 tablespoon minced red onion

PROVENÇAL SALMON

- 1 tablespoon fennel seeds, crushed
- 2 teaspoons Herbes de Provence
- 1 teaspoon freshly grated orange peel
- ¾ teaspoon salt
- 4 salmon steaks, ¾-inch thick (about 6 ounces each)

1 **Prepare Tomato-Olive Relish:** From lemon, grate ½ teaspoon peel and squeeze 1 tablespoon juice. In medium bowl, toss lemon peel and juice with olives, tomato, and onion. Cover and refrigerate relish up to 1 day if not serving right away. Makes about 1¼ cups.

2 Prepare outdoor grill for covered direct grilling over medium heat.

3 **Prepare Provençal Salmon:** In cup, mix fennel seeds, Herbes de Provence, orange peel, and salt. Rub herb mixture on both sides of salmon.

4 Place salmon on hot grill rack over medium heat. Grill until just opaque throughout, about 8 minutes, turning once. Serve salmon with relish.

....

EACH SERVING SALMON: ABOUT 270 CALORIES, 29G PROTEIN, 1G CARBOHYDRATE, 16G TOTAL FAT (3G SATURATED), 80MG CHOLESTEROL, 515MG SODIUM ☺

EACH ¼ CUP RELISH: ABOUT 25 CALORIES, 0G PROTEIN, 3G CARBOHYDRATE, 2G TOTAL FAT (0G SATURATED), 0MG CHOLESTEROL, 330MG SODIUM 🍲

Shrimp SONOMA

Some of the sweetest dried tomatoes we've tried come from the Sonoma Valley in California. Choose dried tomatoes that are plump rather than dry and leathery. Serve on a bed of couscous seasoned with extra-virgin olive oil.

PREP: 25 MINUTES   **GRILL:** 8 TO 10 MINUTES   **MAKES:** 6 MAIN-DISH SERVINGS

1   ounce dried tomatoes without salt

1   cup boiling water

1½ pounds large shrimp

2   tablespoons fresh lemon juice

2   tablespoons olive oil

½   teaspoon salt

½   teaspoon crushed red pepper

4   (12-inch) metal skewers

1 Place dried tomatoes in small bowl. Pour boiling water over tomatoes; let stand while preparing shrimp.

2 Meanwhile, pull off legs from shrimp. Insert tip of kitchen shears under shell of each shrimp and snip along back to tail, cutting about ¼-inch deep to expose dark vein. Leaving shell on, rinse shrimp to remove vein; pat dry with paper towels. Place shrimp in bowl.

3 Prepare outdoor grill for direct grilling over medium heat.

4 Drain dried tomatoes, reserving *¼ cup soaking liquid.*

5 In blender or in food processor with knife blade attached, puree softened tomatoes, reserved soaking liquid, lemon juice, oil, salt, and crushed red pepper until smooth. Pour over shrimp.

6 Thread shrimp onto skewers. Place skewers on hot grill rack over medium heat. Grill shrimp, turning skewers occasionally and basting with any remaining tomato puree, until just opaque throughout, 8 to 10 minutes.

EACH SERVING: ABOUT 140 CALORIES, 20G PROTEIN, 3G CARBOHYDRATE, 5G TOTAL FAT (1G SATURATED), 140MG CHOLESTEROL, 290MG SODIUM ♥ ☺

FISH & SEAFOOD

SCALLOP AND CHERRY
Tomato Skewers

These skewers make for a memorable contrast in flavor and texture—creamy scallops, sweet tart tomatoes, and tangy mustard. Serve with Grilled Caesar Salad (minus the chicken) on page 23.

PREP: 10 MINUTES   **GRILL:** 12 TO 14 MINUTES   **MAKES:** 4 MAIN-DISH SERVINGS

8   (8-inch) bamboo skewers

1   lemon

2   tablespoons olive oil

2   tablespoons Dijon mustard

⅛   teaspoon salt

24 cherry tomatoes

16 large sea scallops (about 1¼ pounds)

1 Soak skewers in hot water at least 30 minutes. Prepare outdoor grill for direct grilling over medium heat.

2 Meanwhile, from lemon, grate 1½ teaspoons peel and squeeze 1 tablespoon juice. In small bowl, whisk lemon peel and juice, oil, mustard, and salt until blended; set aside.

3 Thread 3 tomatoes and 2 scallops alternately on each skewer, beginning and ending with tomatoes.

4 Brush scallops and tomatoes with half of mustard mixture; place on hot grill rack over medium heat. Cook 7 to 9 minutes, turning several times. Brush with remaining mustard mixture and cook until scallops just turn opaque throughout, about 5 minutes longer.

EACH SERVING: ABOUT 215 CALORIES, 25G PROTEIN, 9G CARBOHYDRATE, 9G TOTAL FAT (1G SATURATED), 47MG CHOLESTEROL, 355MG SODIUM 🟢 ❤️ 😊

ASIAN TUNA **Burgers**

Finely chop the fish by hand for a light texture; using a food processor will make the patties dense and dry. Serve with pickled ginger, with or without a bun. Cool Cucumber Relish (page 117) would be the perfect condiment to serve with these tasty burgers.

PREP: 15 MINUTES   **GRILL:** 6 TO 7 MINUTES   **MAKES:** 4 MAIN-DISH SERVINGS

1   tuna steak (about 1 pound)

1   green onion, thinly sliced

2   tablespoons reduced-sodium soy sauce

1   teaspoon grated, peeled fresh ginger

¼   teaspoon coarsely ground black pepper

¼   cup plain dried bread crumbs

2   tablespoons sesame seeds

nonstick cooking spray

1 Prepare outdoor grill for direct grilling over medium heat.

2 With large chef's knife, finely chop tuna and place in medium bowl. Add green onion, soy sauce, ginger, and pepper; mix until combined (mixture will be soft and moist). Shape tuna mixture into four 3-inch round patties.

3 On waxed paper, combine bread crumbs and sesame seeds. With hands, carefully press patties, one at a time, into bread-crumb mixture, turning to coat both sides. Spray both sides of tuna patties with cooking spray.

4 Place patties on hot grill rack over medium heat and grill, turning once, until browned on the outside and still slightly pink in the center for medium-rare or until desired doneness, 6 to 7 minutes.

....

EACH BURGER: ABOUT 210 CALORIES, 26G PROTEIN, 7G CARBOHYDRATE, 8G TOTAL FAT (2G SATURATED), 38MG CHOLESTEROL, 400MG SODIUM 🟢 ❤️ 😊

Salmon BLTs WITH LEMON-DILL MAYONNAISE

Keep the skin on salmon fillets for grilling to prevent them from falling apart. For photo of Salmon BLTs, see page 72.

PREP: 15 MINUTES   **GRILL:** 11 TO 13 MINUTES   **MAKES:** 4 MAIN-DISH SERVINGS

- ⅓ cup light mayonnaise
- 2 teaspoons chopped fresh dill
- 1 teaspoon freshly grated lemon peel
- 4 pieces salmon fillet with skin on, 1-inch thick (about 6 ounces each)
- ¼ teaspoon salt
- ⅛ teaspoon coarsely ground black pepper
- 8 center slices (½-inch thick) country-style bread
- 4 romaine lettuce leaves
- 2 ripe medium tomatoes (6 to 8 ounces each), sliced
- 6 slices bacon, cooked until crisp and each broken in half

1 Lightly grease grill rack. Prepare outdoor grill for covered direct grilling over medium heat.

2 In small bowl, stir mayonnaise, dill, and lemon peel until mixed; set aside. With tweezers, remove any pin bones from salmon. Sprinkle salmon with salt and pepper.

3 Place salmon, skin side down, on hot grill rack over medium heat. Cover grill and cook until salmon is opaque throughout, 10 to 12 minutes, without turning over. Slide thin metal spatula between salmon flesh and skin. Lift salmon from skin and transfer to plate; discard skin if you like. Meanwhile, place bread on grill rack with salmon and cook about 1 minute on each side, until lightly toasted.

4 Spread lemon-dill mayonnaise on 1 side of toasted bread slices. Place 1 lettuce leaf, folding to fit, on each of 4 bread slices. Top each with 2 or 3 tomato slices, 1 salmon fillet, 3 pieces of bacon, and another bread slice.

EACH SERVING: ABOUT 570 CALORIES, 44G PROTEIN, 41G CARBOHYDRATE, 24G TOTAL FAT (5G SATURATED), 108MG CHOLESTEROL, 955MG SODIUM

Miso-Glazed Salmon
WITH EDAMAME SALAD

Spread a mixture of miso, ginger, and cayenne pepper on a large salmon fillet. Enjoy with our healthy soybean salad for a Japanese-inspired meal.

PREP: 30 MINUTES   **GRILL:** 10 TO 12 MINUTES   **MAKES:** 4 MAIN-DISH SERVINGS

EDAMAME SALAD

- 16 ounces frozen shelled edamame (soybeans) or baby lima beans
- 1/4 cup seasoned rice vinegar
- 1 tablespoon vegetable oil
- 1 teaspoon sugar
- 3/4 teaspoon salt
- 1/8 teaspoon coursely ground black pepper
- 1 bunch radishes (8 ounces), each cut in half and thinly sliced
- 1 cup loosely packed fresh cilantro leaves, chopped

MISO-GLAZED SALMON

- 2 tablespoons red miso
- 1 green onion, minced
- 1 tablespoon grated, peeled fresh ginger
- 1 teaspoon brown sugar
- 1/8 teaspoon ground red pepper (cayenne)
- 1 salmon fillet with skin on (about 1½ pounds)

1 Prepare Edamame Salad: Cook edamame as label directs; drain. Rinse edamame with cold running water to stop cooking and drain again.

2 In medium bowl, whisk vinegar, oil, sugar, salt, and pepper until blended. Add edamame, radishes, and cilantro; toss to coat. Cover and refrigerate salad up to 1 day if not serving right away. Makes 4 cups.

3 Prepare outdoor grill for direct grilling over medium-low heat.

4 Prepare Miso-Glazed Salmon: With tweezers, remove any pin bones from salmon. In small bowl, with spoon, mix miso, green onion, ginger, brown sugar, and ground red pepper. Rub miso mixture on flesh side of salmon.

5 Place salmon, skin side down, on hot grill rack and grill until just opaque throughout, 10 to 12 minutes, turning once. Serve with Edamame Salad.

EACH SERVING SALMON: ABOUT 280 CALORIES, 29G PROTEIN, 3G CARBOHYDRATE, 16G TOTAL FAT (3G SATURATED), 80MG CHOLESTEROL, 450MG SODIUM ♥ ☺

EACH 1 CUP SALAD: ABOUT 220 CALORIES, 16G PROTEIN, 23G CARBOHYDRATE, 8G TOTAL FAT (0G SATURATED), 0MG CHOLESTEROL, 1,020MG SODIUM 🗑

A Guide to Buying and Storing Fish

BUYING

• Be sure to shop in a clean, reputable market. Don't buy fish that has a distinct "fishy" odor (fresh fish smells like a sea breeze).

• Make sure fillets and steaks have a shiny, moist, translucent appearance; the flesh should be firm with no gaps between the flakes. There should be no browning or drying around the edges, and no evidence of extra liquid.

• Buying frozen fish? Select a brand that's well wrapped and rock hard, without any freezer burn.

STORING

• Make the fish market your last stop before heading home. To be extra safe on extended rides or on hot days, store fish in a small cooler with a couple of ice packs.

• Store fish in the coldest part of the fridge—either at the back of the bottom shelf or in the meat drawer.

• If keeping overnight, remove the fish from the packaging and pat dry. Cover loosely with plastic wrap and layer the wrapped fish with ice in a colander. Place the colander over a bowl to catch drips.

• Always keep raw seafood away from other foods to avoid cross-contamination, and wash hands and surfaces thoroughly with hot soapy water after handling.

• Plan to use fresh fish right away or, at the very latest, within a day or two. Frozen fish can be kept up to six months.

Grilled Halibut WITH FRESH DILL

If halibut is not available, substitute a firm meaty fish like swordfish or tuna steaks. White-wine Worcestershire sauce is more delicate in flavor than the original Worcestershire and is particularly good with seafood and poultry. If you can't find it, use 2 tablespoons original Worcestershire and add 2 tablespoons water.

PREP: 5 MINUTES PLUS MARINATING   **GRILL:** ABOUT 10 MINUTES   **MAKES:** 4 MAIN-DISH SERVINGS

- ¼   cup white-wine Worcestershire sauce
- 2   tablespoons fresh lemon juice
- 1   tablespoon olive oil
- 1   tablespoon minced fresh dill
- ¼   teaspoon coarsely ground black pepper
- 2   halibut steaks, 1-inch thick (about 12 ounces each)

1 In medium bowl, stir Worcestershire, lemon juice, oil, dill, and pepper. Place halibut in large ziptight plastic bag. Add Worcestershire mixture. Seal bag, pressing out excess air. Place bag on plate; refrigerate up to 2 hours, turning bag over once.

2 Prepare outdoor grill for direct grilling over low heat.

3 Place halibut on hot grill rack, reserving marinade. Grill halibut, turning occasionally and basting frequently with reserved marinade, until opaque throughout, about 10 minutes.

EACH SERVING: ABOUT 195 CALORIES, 29G PROTEIN, 3G CARBOHYDRATE, 7G TOTAL FAT (1G SATURATED), 45MG CHOLESTEROL, 200MG SODIUM 🙂 ❤ ☺

TIP

Stir up an extra batch of the Worcestershire mixture to serve as a sauce for the fish.

Jamaican Jerk Catfish
WITH GRILLED PINEAPPLE

Other fish fillets like snapper and bluefish work well with these zesty flavors too. A versatile seasoning, jerk also does wonders for grilled chicken and pork. Add another jalapeño or some crushed red pepper if you'd like a spicier jerk.

PREP: 15 MINUTES   **GRILL:** 10 TO 12 MINUTES   **MAKES:** 4 MAIN-DISH SERVINGS

2   green onions, chopped

1   jalapeño chile (see tip), seeded and chopped

2   tablespoons white wine vinegar

2   tablespoons Worcestershire sauce

1   tablespoon minced, peeled fresh ginger

1   tablespoon vegetable oil

1¼ teaspoons dried thyme

1   teaspoon ground allspice

¼   teaspoon salt

4   catfish fillets (about 5 ounces each)

1   small pineapple, cut lengthwise into 4 wedges or crosswise into ½-inch-thick slices

2   tablespoons brown sugar

1 Prepare outdoor grill for direct grilling over medium-high heat.

2 In medium bowl, mix green onions, jalapeño, vinegar, Worcestershire, ginger, oil, thyme, allspice, and salt until combined. Add catfish fillets to bowl, turning to coat; let stand 5 minutes at room temperature.

3 Meanwhile, rub pineapple wedges or slices with brown sugar.

4 Place pineapple and catfish fillets on hot grill rack over medium-high heat. Brush half of jerk mixture remaining in bowl on catfish; grill 5 minutes. Turn pineapple and catfish. Brush remaining jerk mixture on fish and grill until fish is just opaque throughout and pineapple is golden brown, 5 to 7 minutes longer.

....

EACH SERVING: ABOUT 350 CALORIES, 23G PROTEIN, 35G CARBOHYDRATE, 14G TOTAL FAT (3G SATURATED), 47MG CHOLESTEROL, 280MG SODIUM 💛 🖤 ☺

TIP

Fresh jalapeño chiles vary in their degree of heat, while pickled jalapeños from a jar are always hot. Feel free to substitute jarred for fresh in most recipes.

Thai Snapper IN FOIL PACKETS

These tender fillets are seasoned with lime and ginger. Don't be tempted to assemble the packets too soon before grilling; the lime juice will start to "cook" the fillets, giving them a mushy texture. Instead, cut the vegetables and prepare the lime juice mixture several hours ahead, but assemble the packets just before cooking.

PREP: 30 MINUTES **GRILL:** 8 MINUTES **MAKES:** 4 MAIN-DISH SERVINGS

- 3 tablespoons fresh lime juice
- 1 tablespoon Asian fish sauce (see tip)
- 1 tablespoon olive oil
- 1 teaspoon grated, peeled fresh ginger
- ½ teaspoon sugar
- ½ teaspoon minced garlic
- 4 (16" by 12") foil sheets
- 4 red snapper fillets (6 ounces each)
- 1 large carrot, peeled and cut into 2¼-inch-long matchstick strips
- 1 large green onion, thinly sliced
- ¼ cup loosely packed fresh cilantro leaves

1 Prepare outdoor grill for direct grilling over medium heat.

2 In small bowl, mix lime juice, fish sauce, oil, ginger, sugar, and garlic.

3 Fold each foil sheet crosswise in half and open up again. Place 1 fillet, skin side down, on one half of each foil sheet. Top each with carrot strips, green onion, and cilantro. Spoon lime juice mixture over snapper and vegetables. Fold unfilled half of foil over fish. To seal packets, beginning at a corner where foil is folded, make small ½-inch folds, with each new fold overlapping previous one, until packet is completely sealed. Packet will resemble half-circle.

4 Place packets on hot grill rack over medium heat; cook 8 minutes.

5 To serve, with kitchen shears, cut an X in top of each packet to allow steam to escape.

EACH SERVING: ABOUT 230 CALORIES, 36G PROTEIN, 5G CARBOHYDRATE, 6G TOTAL FAT (1G SATURATED), 63MG CHOLESTEROL, 270MG SODIUM ♥ ☺

TIP

Asian fish sauce (nuoc nam or nam pla) is a thin, translucent, salty brown liquid extracted from salted, fermented fish. This condiment is used mostly in Thai and Vietnamese cooking. It can be purchased in the Asian sections of most grocery stores.

GRILLED **Fish Tacos**

Coated with a bold, Baja-style rub of cayenne and oregano and then char-crusted on the grill, the tilapia in these taqueria-worthy tacos tastes anything but fishy. A from-scratch salsa with corn and avocado adds to the meal's authenticity.

PREP: 15 MINUTES **GRILL:** ABOUT 10 MINUTES **MAKES:** 4 MAIN-DISH SERVINGS

1 lemon

2½ teaspoons vegetable oil

½ teaspoon plus pinch salt

2 ears corn, husks and silk removed

1 avocado, cut in half and pitted

3 garlic cloves, crushed with garlic press

½ teaspoon dried oregano

¼ teaspoon ground red pepper (cayenne)

1 pound skinless tilapia fillets

12 (6-inch) corn tortillas

1 large ripe tomato (10-12 ounces), finely chopped

Fresh cilantro leaves and lime wedges

1 Prepare outdoor grill for direct grilling over medium-high heat. From lemon, grate 2 teaspoons peel and squeeze 2 tablespoons juice.

2 On plate, rub ½ teaspoon oil and pinch salt all over corn and cut sides of avocado. On another plate, combine garlic, oregano, ground red pepper, lemon peel, ¼ teaspoon salt, and remaining 2 teaspoons oil. Place fish on plate and rub mixture all over to coat.

3 Place fish, corn, and avocado, cut sides down, on hot grill rack. Cook fish until opaque through-out, 3 to 4 minutes, turning once; cook vegetables until charred, about 5 minutes, turning occasionally.

4 Transfer fish, corn, and avocado to cutting board. Let cool while warming tortillas: Place tortillas on grill in single layer and cook 1 minute, turning once. Stack on large sheet of foil and wrap tightly.

5 Cut kernels from corn cobs. Peel and finely chop avocado. Break fish into large chunks. In large bowl, mix together tomato, corn, avocado, lemon juice, and remaining ¼ teaspoon salt. Divide fish and tomato mixture among tortillas and serve with cilantro and lime wedges.

EACH SERVING: ABOUT 420 CALORIES, 31G PROTEIN, 49G CARBOHYDRATE, 13G TOTAL FAT (2G SATURATED), 9G FIBER, 52MG CHOLESTEROL, 425MG SODIUM ♥ ♥ ☺

TIP

Flounder, catfish, or any mild white fish would be a good substitute for the tilapia. Grill fish fillets only 8 to 10 minutes per inch of thickness.

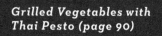

Grilled Vegetables with Thai Pesto (page 90)

5 Vegetables & Meatless Mains

Grilling turns simple vegetables into the stars of the plate. Smoke and heat concentrate flavors and add depth to everything from corn to zucchini.

Thai pesto marries flavors of basil, sweet chili sauce and lime to serve as the sauce for an assortment of grilled veggies. Bread crumbs top halved plum tomatoes, and polenta rounds overflow with Fontina cheese. All these, along with our handy guide on cooking times for every vegetable imaginable, give you options for pairing veggies in any grilled meat, or promoting these combos to the center of the dinner plate.

For meatless dinners, turn to Black-Bean Burgers topped with smoky chipotle mayonnaise or Hoisin-Grilled Tofu and Vegetables. Pizzas slathered with pesto and mozzarella are single-serve and grill-roasted bell peppers are the centerpiece for grilled burritos.

KEY TO ICONS

◐ 30 MINUTES OR LESS   ♥ HEART HEALTHY   ☺ LOW CALORIE   🍱 MAKE AHEAD

Grilled Vegetables
WITH THAI PESTO

Pesto takes a Thai-inspired twist when we add fresh lime and sweet chili sauce to the mix. Turn it into dinner with Cool Cucumber Relish, page 117, and a side of rice. For photo, see page 88.

PREP: 20 MINUTES   **GRILL:** 10 TO 12 MINUTES   **MAKES:** 4 SIDE-DISH SERVINGS

THAI PESTO

1   large lime

½   cup walnuts

1   cup packed fresh basil leaves

1   tablespoon Thai sweet chili sauce

3   tablespoons water

¼   teaspoon salt

GRILLED VEGETABLES

olive oil or nonstick cooking spray

4   plum tomatoes, each cut lengthwise in half

2   medium yellow peppers, each cut into quarters, seeded, and stemmed

½   medium (1½ to 2 pounds) eggplant, cut crosswise into ¾-inch-thick slices

1   large zucchini (about 10 ounces), cut diagonally into ½-inch-thick slices

½   large sweet onion (12 ounces), cut through root end into 6 wedges

¼   teaspoon salt

1 Prepare Thai Pesto: From lime, grate ½ teaspoon peel and squeeze 2 tablespoons juice. In skillet, toast walnuts over medium heat 5 minutes, stirring, until fragrant. Set aside.

2 In food processor with knife blade attached, blend nuts, basil, chili sauce, water, lime peel and juice, and salt. Store covered in refrigerator up to 2 days. Makes about ⅔ cup.

3 Prepare Grilled Vegetables: Prepare outdoor grill for covered direct grilling over medium heat, or heat large ridged grill pan over medium until hot. Lightly spray vegetables with cooking spray. Place vegetables on hot grill rack or pan. Cover grill and cook tomatoes and zucchini 6 to 8 minutes, peppers and onion 8 to 10 minutes, and eggplant 10 to 12 minutes or until vegetables are tender, turning once. Transfer vegetables to serving plate as they are done; sprinkle with salt. Serve with Thai Pesto.

EACH SERVING: ABOUT 205 CALORIES, 6G PROTEIN, 26G CARBOHYDRATE, 11G TOTAL FAT (1G SATURATED), 7G FIBER, 0MG CHOLESTEROL, 365MG SODIUM

GRILLED VEGETABLE **Burritos**

To make this all-in-one entrée, roll grilled onion, peppers, and zucchini in tortillas with shredded cheeses. If you prefer your burritos mild, substitute Monterey Jack without jalapeño chiles or use all Cheddar cheese. Serve with your favorite jarred salsa and a dollop of sour cream.

PREP: 25 MINUTES   **GRILL:** 16 TO 21 MINUTES   **MAKES:** 4 MAIN-DISH SERVINGS

1   tablespoon plus 1 teaspoon vegetable oil

1   teaspoon chili powder

1   teaspoon ground cumin

½   teaspoon salt

¼   teaspoon coursely ground black pepper

2   medium zucchini (about 10 ounces each), cut lengthwise into ¼-inch-thick slices

1   large onion (12 ounces), cut into ½-inch-thick slices

1   medium red pepper, stem and seeds removed, cut into quarters

1   medium green pepper, stem and seeds removed, cut into quarters

4   (10-inch) flour tortillas

2   ounces sharp Cheddar cheese, shredded (½ cup)

2   ounces Monterey Jack cheese with jalapeño chiles, shredded (½ cup)

½   cup loosely packed fresh cilantro leaves

jarred salsa and sour cream (optional)

1 Prepare outdoor grill for covered direct grilling over medium heat.

2 In small bowl, mix oil, chili powder, cumin, salt, and black pepper. Brush one side of zucchini, onion, and red and green pepper with oil mixture.

3 Place vegetables, oiled side down, on hot grill rack over medium heat and grill, turning once and transferring vegetables to plate as they are done, until tender and golden, 15 to 20 minutes.

4 Arrange one-fourth of grilled vegetables down center of each tortilla; sprinkle with Cheddar and Monterey Jack cheeses. Place open burritos on grill rack. Cover grill and cook until cheeses melt, about 1 minute.

5 Transfer burritos to plates. Sprinkle cilantro over cheese, then fold sides of tortillas over filling. Serve with salsa and sour cream, if you like.

....

EACH SERVING: ABOUT 330 CALORIES, 11G PROTEIN, 43G CARBOHYDRATE, 14G TOTAL FAT (4G SATURATED), 15MG CHOLESTEROL, 655MG SODIUM ☺

Grilled Eggplant PARMESAN

Grilling gives eggplant a smoky flavor and eliminating the frying makes this outdoor version of Eggplant Parmesan light and fresh tasting. Use freshly grated Parmesan cheese and the ripest summer tomatoes you can find for this flavorful twist on the traditional dish.

PREP: 25 MINUTES   **GRILL:** 11 TO 14 MINUTES   **MAKES:** 4 SIDE-DISH OR 2 MAIN-DISH SERVINGS

1   medium-large eggplant (about 1½ pounds), cut lengthwise into 4 slices

1   tablespoon plus 1 teaspoon olive oil

½   teaspoon salt

¼   teaspoon coarsely ground black pepper

4   ounces mozzarella cheese, shredded (1 cup)

¼   cup freshly grated Parmesan cheese

½   cup loosely packed fresh basil leaves, thinly sliced

2   ripe medium tomatoes (6 to 8 ounces each), each cut into 4 slices

1 Prepare outdoor grill for covered direct grilling over medium heat.

2 Lightly brush eggplant slices with oil and sprinkle with salt and pepper. In small bowl, mix mozzarella, Parmesan, and basil; set aside.

3 Place eggplant slices on hot grill rack over medium heat and grill, turning once, until tender and lightly browned, 10 to 12 minutes. Top with tomato slices and cheese mixture. Cover grill and cook until cheese melts and tomato slices are warm, 1 to 2 minutes.

EACH SIDE-DISH SERVING: ABOUT 205 CALORIES, 10G PROTEIN, 15G CARBOHYDRATE, 13G TOTAL FAT (5G SATURATED), 26MG CHOLESTEROL, 500MG SODIUM

A Guide to Grilled Vegetables

Preheat the grill to medium-high.

VEGETABLE	PREPARATION	SEASONING	GRILLING TIME
8 ears corn	Soak 15 minutes, then remove silk from tops only or remove husks and silk.	Brush with 1 tablespoon oil.	20–30 minutes with husks; 12–15 minutes, turning occasionally, without husks
1½-pound eggplant	Cut crosswise into ½-inch-thick slices.	Brush with ¼ cup oil.	11–13 minutes per side
4 heads Belgian endive	Cut lengthwise in half.	Brush with 1 tablespoon oil.	10–12 minutes per side
2 medium fennel bulbs (1 pound each)	Cut lengthwise into ¼-inch-thick slices.	Brush with 4 teaspoons oil.	6–8 minutes per side
6 medium leeks	Remove dark green tops; blanch and halve lengthwise.	Toss with 1 tablespoon oil.	11–13 minutes per side
8 ounces large white mushrooms	Trim and thread onto skewers.	Brush with 2 teaspoons oil.	20 minutes per side, turning several times
4 large portobello mushrooms	Remove stems.	Brush with 4 teaspoons oil.	15 minutes per side
4 medium red or white onions	Slice into ½-inch-thick slices; secure with skewers.	Brush with 4 teaspoons oil.	12–14 minutes per side
2 bunches small green onions	Trim root ends and tops.	Toss with 4 teaspoons oil.	2–4 minutes, turning several times
4 red, green, or yellow peppers	Cut lengthwise into quarters; discard seeds.		10–12 minutes per side
4 medium yellow squash or zucchini	Cut lengthwise into ¼-inch-thick slices.	Brush with 4 teaspoons oil.	5 minutes per side
4 medium tomatoes (6 to 8 ounces each)	Cut crosswise in half.	Brush cut sides with 2 tablespoons oil.	14–17 minutes per side

CRUMB-TOPPED **Tomatoes**

To make last minute prep even easier, you can brown the bread crumbs up to a day ahead and refrigerate. Swap in basil for the parsley if you prefer.

PREP: 15 MINUTES   **GRILL:** 8 TO 10 MINUTES   **MAKES:** 8 SIDE-DISH SERVINGS

2 tablespoons butter or trans-fat free margarine

1 cup fresh bread crumbs (about 2 slices firm white bread)

1 garlic clove, crushed with garlic press

2 tablespoons chopped fresh parsley

½ teaspoon salt

½ teaspoon coarsely ground black pepper

8 ripe large plum tomatoes

1 Prepare outdoor grill for direct grilling over medium heat.

2 In 10-inch skillet, melt butter over low heat. Add bread crumbs and cook, stirring, until lightly browned. Stir in garlic; cook 30 seconds. Remove skillet from heat; stir in parsley, salt, and pepper.

3 Cut each tomato horizontally in half. Top each tomato half with some crumb mixture. Place tomatoes on hot grill rack over medium heat, crumb side up, and grill until hot but not mushy, 8 to 10 minutes.

....

EACH SERVING: ABOUT 40 CALORIES, 1G PROTEIN, 3G CARBOHYDRATE, 3G TOTAL FAT (2G SATURATED), 8MG CHOLESTEROL, 191MG SODIUM 🗨 ♥ ☺

TIP

To make fresh bread crumbs, tear bread into large pieces and process in a food processor with the knife blade attached to form crumbs.

FLAME-ROASTED **Chiles Relleños**

Prep these chiles in the morning, rub steak chicken or pork with our spicy rub on page 55, and sit back until grilling time. If you prefer hotter flavor, after grilling and before filling the chiles, remove the seeds and veins but don't rinse the insides.

PREP: 20 MINUTES   **GRILL:** 20 TO 25 MINUTES PLUS STEAMING   **MAKES:** 6 SIDE-DISH SERVINGS

6   medium poblano chiles (about 4 ounces each)

6   ounces Monterey Jack cheese, shredded (1½ cups)

1   cup corn kernels cut from cobs (about 2 medium ears)

½   cup loosely packed fresh cilantro leaves, chopped

1 Prepare outdoor grill for direct grilling over medium heat.

2 Place whole chiles on hot grill rack and cook, turning occasionally, until blistered and blackened on all sides, 10 to 15 minutes.

3 Transfer chiles to large sheet of foil. Wrap them, seal tightly, and allow to steam at room temperature until cool enough to handle, about 15 minutes.

4 Meanwhile, in medium bowl, combine cheese, corn, and cilantro.

5 Remove chiles from foil. Cut 2-inch lengthwise slit in side of each chile, being careful not to cut through top or bottom. Under cold running water, gently peel off skin. Remove seeds and veins from opening; rinse with running water. Pat chiles dry with paper towels.

6 With spoon, fill each chile with about ½ cup cheese mixture. Gently reshape chiles to close opening. Place 3 filled chiles in single layer on each of two 18-inch square sheets of heavy-duty foil. Bring two sides of foil up and fold several times to seal. Fold over ends to seal in juices. (Chiles can be prepared to this point and refrigerated up to 6 hours before grilling.)

7 Place foil packet on hot grill rack over medium heat and cook until heated through and cheese has melted, about 10 minutes.

EACH SERVING: ABOUT 160 CALORIES, 9G PROTEIN, 13G CARBOHYDRATE, 9G TOTAL FAT (5G SATURATED), 30MG CHOLESTEROL, 160MG SODIUM

HOISIN-GRILLED
Tofu and Vegetables

This gingery glaze adds sweet heat to tofu, zucchini, and red pepper. Be sure to buy extra-firm tofu; other varieties will fall apart during grilling.

PREP: 25 MINUTES   **GRILL:** ABOUT 11 MINUTES   **MAKES:** 4 MAIN-DISH SERVINGS

HOISIN-GINGER GLAZE

- ½ cup hoisin sauce
- 2 garlic cloves, crushed with garlic press
- 1 tablespoon vegetable oil
- 1 tablespoon reduced-sodium soy sauce
- 1 tablespoon grated, peeled fresh ginger
- 1 tablespoon seasoned rice vinegar
- ⅛ teaspoon ground red pepper (cayenne)

TOFU AND VEGGIES

- 1 package (15 ounces) extra-firm tofu
- 2 medium zucchini (about 10 ounces each), each cut lengthwise into quarters and then crosswise in half
- 1 large red pepper, cut lengthwise into quarters, stem and seeds discarded
- 1 bunch green onions, trimmed
- 1 teaspoon vegetable oil

1 Prepare outdoor grill for direct grilling over medium heat.

2 **Prepare Hoisin-Ginger Glaze:** In small bowl, with fork, mix hoisin sauce, garlic, oil, soy sauce, ginger, vinegar, and ground red pepper until well blended.

3 **Prepare Tofu and Veggies:** Cut tofu horizontally into 4 pieces, then cut each piece crosswise in half. Place tofu on paper towels; pat dry with additional paper towels. Arrange tofu on large plate and brush both sides of tofu with half of glaze. Spoon remaining half of glaze into medium bowl; add zucchini and red pepper. Gently toss vegetables to coat with glaze. On another plate, rub green onions with oil.

4 Grill tofu, zucchini, and red peppers, gently turning once with wide metal spatula, 6 minutes. Transfer tofu to platter; keep warm. Continue cooking vegetables, transferring them to platter with tofu as they are done, until tender and browned, about 5 minutes longer.

5 Grill green onions during last minute of cooking time; transfer to platter.

EACH SERVING: ABOUT 245 CALORIES, 15G PROTEIN, 22G CARBOHYDRATE, 11G TOTAL FAT (1G SATURATED), 0MG CHOLESTEROL, 615MG SODIUM ☺

Grilled Polenta WITH FONTINA

Simple side! Slice a log of precooked polenta from the supermarket. Add melted cheese and chopped tomatoes for a tasty topping.

PREP: 10 MINUTES   **GRILL:** ABOUT 10 MINUTES   **MAKES:** 6 SIDE-DISH SERVINGS

2   ripe medium tomatoes (6 to 8 ounces each), chopped

2   tablespoons chopped fresh parsley

1/4   teaspoon salt

1/8   teaspoon coarsely ground black pepper

1   package (24 ounces) precooked polenta, cut into 12 slices

1   tablespoon olive oil

2   ounces Fontina cheese, shredded (1/2 cup; see tip)

1 Prepare outdoor grill for direct grilling over medium heat.

2 In small bowl, combine tomatoes, parsley, salt, and pepper; set aside.

3 Brush both sides of polenta slices with oil. Place polenta slices on hot grill rack over medium heat and grill until undersides are golden, about 5 minutes. Turn slices and top with cheese. Grill polenta just until cheese melts, about 5 minutes longer.

4 Transfer polenta slices to platter and top with tomato mixture.

. . . .

EACH SERVING: ABOUT 150 CALORIES, 5G PROTEIN, 19G CARBOHYDRATE, 5G TOTAL FAT (2G SATURATED), 11MG CHOLESTEROL, 380MG SODIUM ✓ ☺

TIP

Can't find Fontina? Substitute Monterey Jack or Muenster cheese. If you'd like to save time, top the grilled polenta with a drizzle of store-bought pesto or salsa instead of our fresh tomato topping.

BLACK-BEAN **Burgers**

This south-of-the-border burger proves that beef-free doesn't have to be bland: Spiced with coriander and cumin, and capped with chile-spiked Tex-Mex mayo, it's as fiery as it is filling.

PREP: 10 MINUTES   **GRILL:** 10 TO 12 MINUTES   **MAKES:** 4 MAIN-DISH SERVINGS

¼ cup dried bread crumbs

¼ teaspoon ground cumin

¼ teaspoon ground coriander

3 cups cooked or 2 cans (15 ounces each) low-sodium black beans, rinsed and drained

4 tablespoons light mayonnaise

¼ teaspoon salt

¼ teaspoon coarsely ground black pepper

2 large stalks celery, finely chopped

1 chipotle chile in adobo, finely chopped

4 green-leaf lettuce leaves

4 whole-wheat hamburger buns, toasted

4 slices ripe tomato

1 In food processor with knife blade attached, pulse bread crumbs, cumin, coriander, two-thirds of beans, 2 tablespoons mayonnaise, salt, and pepper until well blended. Transfer to large bowl. Stir in celery and remaining whole beans until well combined. Divide mixture into 4 equal portions and shape into patties.

2 Prepare outdoor grill for direct grilling over medium heat, or heat large ridged grill pan over medium heat until hot. Add burgers and cook until lightly browned and heated through, 10 to 12 minutes, turning them once.

3 Meanwhile, in small bowl, combine chipotle chile and remaining 2 tablespoons mayonnaise until well mixed. Place 1 lettuce leaf on bottom of each bun; top with patty, then tomato slice. Divide chipotle mayonnaise among burgers and replace tops of buns to serve.

EACH BURGER: ABOUT 370 CALORIES, 18G PROTEIN, 59G CARBOHYDRATE, 8G TOTAL FAT (1G SATURATED), 14G FIBER, 5MG CHOLESTEROL, 725MG SODIUM ☺

PESTO AND MOZZARELLA **Pizzas**

Garden tomatoes and basil make a wonderful topping for pizza cooked over the coals. Serve as a main course or cut into wedges for appetizers.

PREP: 25 MINUTES   **GRILL:** 4 TO 6 MINUTES   **MAKES:** 4 PIZZAS OR 4 MAIN-DISH SERVINGS

nonstick cooking spray

1   pound refrigerated fresh pizza dough from supermarket or pizzeria, at room temperature

¼   cup jarred pesto sauce

3   plum tomatoes, seeded and chopped

8   ounces fresh mozzarella cheese, thinly sliced

½   teaspoon coarsely ground black pepper

1 Prepare outdoor grill for covered direct grilling over medium heat.

2 Meanwhile, spray 2 large cookie sheets with cooking spray. On work surface, divide dough into 4 equal pieces; spray with cooking spray. With fingertips, press each piece of dough into a round about ⅛ inch thick (it's OK if dough is not perfectly round). Or, if necessary, with rolling pin, roll each dough piece to ⅛-inch thickness. Transfer 2 rounds to each prepared cookie sheet; cover loosely with plastic wrap. (Bring dough rounds and remaining ingredients to grill for final pizza assembly.)

3 Place dough rounds on hot grill rack over medium heat. Cover grill and cook until grill marks appear on underside and dough stiffens (dough may puff slightly), 2 to 3 minutes. With tongs, carefully transfer dough to same cookie sheets, grill-marks side up.

4 Spread pesto on grilled side of dough rounds; top with tomatoes, mozzarella, and pepper.

5 Return dough rounds to grill, toppings side up. Cover grill and cook pizzas until bottom of dough stiffens and mozzarella begins to melt, 2 to 3 minutes longer. Transfer pizzas to cutting board; cut into wedges to serve.

EACH SERVING: ABOUT 530 CALORIES, 19G PROTEIN, 59G CARBOHYDRATE, 24G TOTAL FAT (9G SATURATED), 3G FIBER, 47MG CHOLESTEROL, 275MG SODIUM 🗸 🗄

MONTEREY JACK PIZZAS

Prepare recipe as in steps 1, 2, and 3 of Pesto and Mozzarella Pizzas. In step 4, spread **1 cup prepared black-bean dip** on grilled side of dough rounds; top with **1 cup shredded Monterey Jack or pepper Jack cheese (4 ounces).** Finish cooking as in step 5. Transfer pizzas to cutting board; top with **2 cups thinly sliced iceberg lettuce** and **½ cup of your favorite salsa.** Cut into wedges to serve.

....

EACH SERVING MONTEREY JACK PIZZA: ABOUT 440 CALORIES, 17G PROTEIN, 64G CARBOHYDRATE, 12G TOTAL FAT (5G SATURATED), 5G FIBER, 25MG CHOLESTEROL 1,080MG SODIUM 🗸 ☺

Corn on the Cob
WITH MOLASSES BUTTER

Ground red pepper and coriander add kick to this molasses-sweetened butter.

PREP: 10 MINUTES   **GRILL:** 12 TO 15 MINUTES   **MAKES:** 8 SIDE-DISH SERVINGS

2 tablespoon butter or trans-fat free margarine, softened

1 teaspoon light (mild) molasses

½ teaspoon ground coriander

½ teaspoon salt

pinch ground red pepper (cayenne)

8 ears corn, husks and silk removed

1 Prepare outdoor grill for covered direct grilling over medium-high heat.

2 In small bowl, with fork, stir butter, molasses, coriander, salt, and ground red pepper until well combined.

3 Place corn on hot grill rack over medium-high heat. Cover grill and cook corn, turning frequently, until brown in spots, 12 to 15 minutes.

4 Transfer corn to platter; spread each ear with molasses butter.

EACH SERVING: ABOUT 105 CALORIES, 3G PROTEIN, 18G CARBOHYDRATE, 4G TOTAL FAT (2G SATURATED), 8MG CHOLESTEROL, 186MG SODIUM 💚 🖤 ☺

LEMON-GARLIC **Potato Packet**

For maximum flavor and minimum fuss, try enclosing your veggies in aluminum foil pouches. They seal in seasoning so you won't have to stand over the coals, basting and glazing. Potatoes are a wonderful choice, but squash and peppers work equally well.

PREP: 15 MINUTES   **GRILL:** 30 MINUTES   **MAKES:** 8 SIDE-DISH SERVINGS

2½ pounds red potatoes, unpeeled and cut into 1-inch chunks

12 garlic cloves, peeled

2 tablespoons olive oil

1½ teaspoons freshly grated lemon peel

1 teaspoon salt

¼ teaspoon coarsely ground black pepper

1 Prepare outdoor grill for covered direct grilling over medium heat.

2 In large bowl, toss potatoes, garlic, oil, lemon peel, salt, and pepper until potatoes are evenly coated.

3 Layer two 30" by 18" sheets of heavy-duty foil on work surface to make double-thick sheet. Place potato mixture in center of stacked foil. Bring short ends of foil up and over potatoes; fold several times to seal. Fold remaining sides of foil several times to seal in juices.

4 Place packet on hot grill rack over medium heat and cook, turning packet over halfway through grilling, until potatoes are fork-tender, 30 minutes.

5 Before serving, with kitchen shears, cut an X in top of foil packet to let steam escape, then carefully pull back foil to open.

EACH SERVING: ABOUT 140 CALORIES, 3G PROTEIN, 25G CARBOHYDRATE, 4G TOTAL FAT (1G SATURATED), 0MG CHOLESTEROL, 275MG SODIUM ♥ ☺

SHALLOT AND HERB POTATO PACKET

Prepare Lemon-Garlic Potato Packets as directed but omit garlic. Add **2 medium shallots**, thinly sliced, and **2 teaspoons minced fresh thyme or ½ teaspoon dried thyme.** Wrap in foil and grill as directed. Before serving, sprinkle with ⅓ **cup chopped fresh parsley.**

....

EACH SERVING: ABOUT 140 CALORIES, 3G PROTEIN, 25G CARBOHYDRATE, 4G TOTAL FAT (1G SATURATED), 0MG CHOLESTEROL, 280MG SODIUM ♥ ☺

Three-Ingredient Side Dishes

Whatever the star attraction on the grill, these simple, speedy sides shine in supporting roles.

BARBECUE BEANS

Chop **3 slices cooked bacon** and place in small saucepan. Add **1 can (28 ounces) baked beans** and ⅓ **cup bottled barbecue sauce**. Cook over medium-low heat to thicken slightly and blend flavors, about 10 minutes. Makes 6 side-dish servings.

GREEN BEAN AND RED PEPPER SALAD

Trim ends from **12 ounces green beans**. Cook in simmering water until tender-crisp, 5 to 10 minutes. Rinse under cold water and drain well. Cut peppers from **1 jar (7 ounces) roasted red peppers** into long strips. In bowl, toss beans, peppers, and **¼ cup bottled balsamic vinaigrette**. Makes 4 side-dish servings.

TOMATO-FETA SALAD

Cut **3 medium ripe tomatoes** into ½-inch chunks. Chop **¼ cup pitted kalamata olives.** In bowl, toss tomatoes, olives, and **½ cup crumbled feta cheese**. Makes 4 side-dish servings.

CORN AND ZUCCHINI SAUTÉ

From **jar of oil-packed dried tomatoes in oil**, sliver enough tomatoes to equal 2 tablespoons. Transfer 1 teaspoon of the oil to large nonstick skillet and heat over medium-high heat. Add **2 medium zucchini,** cut into ¼-inch-thick half-moons, and cook 4 minutes. Stir in **2 cups fresh corn kernels** (from about 4 ears), the slivered tomatoes, and **½ teaspoon salt**; cook 4 minutes or until vegetables are tender-crisp. Makes 6 side-dish servings.

MARINATED BROCCOLI SALAD

Cook **4 cups broccoli florets** (8 ounces) in simmering water until tender-crisp, about 10 minutes. Rinse and drain well. In bowl, toss broccoli, **8 ounces marinated bocconcini** (small fresh mozzarella balls), and 3 tablespoons bocconcini marinade with **2 tablespoons fresh lemon juice.** Makes 4 side-dish servings.

EASY POTATO SALAD

In saucepan, combine **1½ pounds small red potatoes** and enough water to cover. Heat to boiling; reduce heat and simmer until potatoes are fork-tender, about 15 minutes. Rinse potatoes under cold water and drain well. Cut into 1-inch chunks and place in bowl; stir in ⅓ **cup bottled creamy Italian dressing** and **½ cup chopped fresh basil**. Makes 6 side-dish servings.

Salsa Fresca, Pineapple-Tomato Salsa, and Green Tomato Salsa (pages 112-113)

6 Salsas, Sauces & Rubs

For those times you're doing simple on the grill and want to spruce it up, we have a variety of salsas and sauces for the choosing. Pineapple-Tomato or Peach Salsa offer a cooling, spicy counterpart to grilled chicken. Grilled fish can be rolled into tortillas and topped with Avocado Pico de Gallo for fish tacos, any steak will benefit from the vibrant, herby Chimichurri Sauce.

Choose your sauce for any rib-slathering needs: Chunky Barbecue Sauce is piqued with ginger or the Secret-Recipe Barbecue Sauce gets a touch of sweet and tart from pineapple. Shrimp can be slathered with herb-based rubs for a quick and easy flavor boost. Or dip a flank steak into a Soy Marinade, and baste chicken with Honey-Mustard Glaze. This chapter offers easy flavor options to match any grill creations.

‖KEY TO ICONS‖

⊘ 30 MINUTES OR LESS   ♥ HEART HEALTHY   ☺ LOW CALORIE   🍲 MAKE AHEAD

Salsa FRESCA

Put summer tomatoes to good use in this lively salsa. For photo of Salsa Fresca, Green Tomato Salsa, and Pineapple-Tomato Salsa, see page 110.

TOTAL TIME: 10 MINUTES PLUS CHILLING   **MAKES:** ABOUT 3 CUPS

1   pound ripe tomatoes (3 medium), chopped

¼   cup chopped sweet onion

¼   cup loosely packed fresh cilantro leaves, chopped

2   tablespoons fresh lime juice

1   jalapeño chile, seeded and minced

½   teaspoon salt

⅛   teaspoon coarsely ground black pepper

In bowl, gently stir tomatoes with onion, cilantro, lime juice, jalapeño, salt, and pepper. Cover and refrigerate at least 1 hour to blend flavors, or up to 8 hours. Drain before serving if chilled longer than 1 hour.

EACH ¼ CUP: ABOUT 10 CALORIES, 0G PROTEIN, 2G CARBOHYDRATE, 0G TOTAL FAT, 1G FIBER, 0MG CHOLESTEROL, 100MG SODIUM 🍲

GREEN TOMATO Salsa

This mild two-tomato salsa amps the sweet flavor of fresh corn.

TOTAL TIME: 15 MINUTES PLUS CHILLING   **MAKES:** ABOUT 3 CUPS

8   ounces green tomatoes (2 small), chopped

8   ounces ripe red tomatoes (2 small), chopped

1   cup fresh corn kernels

¼   cup snipped fresh chives

2   tablespoons fresh lemon juice

½   teaspoon salt

⅛   teaspoon coarsely ground black pepper

In medium bowl, gently stir tomatoes with corn, chives, lemon juice, salt, and pepper. Cover and refrigerate at least 1 hour to blend flavors, or up to 8 hours. Drain before serving if chilled longer than 1 hour.

EACH ¼ CUP: ABOUT 20 CALORIES, 0G PROTEIN, 4G CARBOHYDRATE, 0G TOTAL FAT, 1G FIBER, 0MG CHOLESTEROL, 90MG SODIUM 🍲

PINEAPPLE-TOMATO **Salsa**

Sweet pineapple and fresh tarragon mingle in this unusually delicious tomato salsa.

TOTAL TIME: 5 MINUTES PLUS CHILLING **MAKES:** ABOUT 4 CUPS

1 pound ripe tomatoes (3 medium), chopped

2 cups chopped fresh pineapple

1 tablespoon fresh lemon juice

2 teaspoons chopped fresh tarragon

½ teaspoon salt

⅛ teaspoon coarsely ground black pepper

In medium bowl, gently stir tomatoes with pineapple, lemon juice, tarragon, salt, and pepper. Cover and refrigerate at least 1 hour to blend flavors, or up to 8 hours. Drain before serving if chilled longer than 1 hour.

EACH ¼ CUP: ABOUT 15 CALORIES, 0G PROTEIN, 4G CARBOHYDRATE, 0G TOTAL FAT, 1G FIBER, 0MG CHOLESTEROL, 75MG SODIUM

PEACH **Salsa**

Be patient. Wait until it is the height of peach season to make this sweet-hot salsa. Spoon over grilled chicken.

TOTAL TIME: 30 MINUTES PLUS CHILLING **MAKES:** ABOUT 3 CUPS

1¾ pounds ripe peaches (5 medium), peeled, pitted, and chopped

2 tablespoons finely chopped red onion

1 tablespoon chopped fresh mint

1 teaspoon seeded, minced jalapeño chile

1 tablespoon fresh lime juice

⅛ teaspoon salt

In medium bowl, combine peaches, onion, mint, jalapeño, lime juice, and salt. Cover and refrigerate for 1 hour to blend flavors or up to 2 days.

EACH ¼ CUP: ABOUT 25 CALORIES, 0G PROTEIN, 6G CARBOHYDRATE, 0G TOTAL FAT, 0MG CHOLESTEROL, 25MG SODIUM

AVOCADO **Pico de Gallo**

Enjoy this fresh, flavorful mix as a topping for grilled chicken or fish. It's also a diet-friendly dipper for sliced vegetables or baked tortilla chips.

TOTAL TIME: 15 MINUTES   **MAKES:** ABOUT 2¾ CUPS

2	medium ripe avocados, peeled, pitted, and cut into ½-inch chunks
3	plum tomatoes, seeded and coarsely chopped
1	jalapeño chile, chopped
⅓	cup chopped sweet onion
¼	cup loosely packed fresh cilantro leaves, chopped
2	tablespoons fresh lime juice
½	teaspoon kosher salt

In medium bowl, combine avocados, tomatoes, jalapeño, onion, cilantro, lime juice, and salt. Store covered in the refrigerator up to 4 hours.

EACH ¼ CUP: ABOUT 60 CALORIES, 1G PROTEIN, 4G CARBOHYDRATE, 5G TOTAL FAT (1G SATURATED), 2G FIBER, 0MG CHOLESTEROL, 95MG SODIUM

Chimichurri SAUCE

This tasty green sauce, thick with fresh herbs, is as common in Argentina as ketchup is in the United States. It's great drizzled over grilled meat and poultry. You can even use it as a salad dressing.

TOTAL TIME: 15 MINUTES   **MAKES:** ABOUT ¼ CUP

1½ cups loosely packed fresh parsley leaves, finely chopped

1½ cups loosely packed fresh cilantro leaves, finely chopped

¼ cup olive oil

3 tablespoons red wine vinegar

1 garlic clove, crushed with garlic press

¼ teaspoon coarsely ground black pepper

¼ teaspoon salt

In small bowl, mix parsley, cilantro, oil, vinegar, garlic, pepper, and salt. Cover and refrigerate up to 2 days if not using right away.

EACH TABLESPOON: ABOUT 65 CALORIES, 0G PROTEIN 1G CARBOHYDRATE, 7G TOTAL FAT (1G SATURATED), 0MG CHOLESTEROL, 70MG SODIUM

Guacamole

Here's everyone's favorite quesadilla and taco topper.

TOTAL TIME: 20 MINUTES   **MAKES:** ABOUT 3 CUPS

2 medium ripe avocados (about 8 ounces each), peeled, pitted, and cut into 1-inch chunks

2 ripe medium tomatoes (about 10 ounces), coarsely chopped

1 jalapeño chile, seeded and minced

1 cup loosely packed fresh cilantro leaves, chopped

1 tablespoon fresh lime juice

½ teaspoon salt

In medium bowl, gently mash avocados, cilantro, lime juice, and salt until well combined. Cover with plastic wrap and refrigerate up to 2 hours.

EACH TABLESPOON: ABOUT 15 CALORIES, 0G PROTEIN, 1G CARBOHYDRATE, 1G TOTAL FAT (0G SATURATED), 0G FIBER, 0MG CHOLESTEROL, 25MG SODIUM

COOL CUCUMBER **Relish**

This is refreshing paired with Gingered Chicken and Beef Saté (page 20) or served alongside grilled fish.

TOTAL TIME: 10 MINUTES   **MAKES:** ABOUT 2½ CUP

4   medium Kirby cucumbers (about 4 ounces each), cut into ¼-inch pieces

¼   cup seasoned rice vinegar

2   tablespoons chopped red onion

1   tablespoon vegetable oil

¼   teaspoon crushed red pepper

In medium bowl, with spoon, combine cucumbers, vinegar, onion, oil, and crushed red pepper. Cover and refrigerate until ready to serve.

EACH ¼ CUP: ABOUT 25 CALORIES | 0G PROTEIN | 3G CARBOHYDRATE | 1G TOTAL FAT (0G SATURATED) | 0MG CHOLESTEROL | 120MG SODIUM

CHUNKY **Barbecue Sauce**

Brush it on pork, chicken, or tofu—this basic sauce will keep in the refrigerator up to one week or in the freezer up to two months.

ACTIVE TIME: 10 MINUTES   **TOTAL TIME:** 30 MINUTES   **MAKES:** ABOUT 4 CUPS

1   tablespoon vegetable oil

1   large onion (12 ounces), chopped

3   garlic cloves, minced

2   tablespoons minced, peeled fresh ginger

1   teaspoon ground cumin

1   can (14 ounces) tomatoes in puree, chopped,

1   bottle (12 ounces) chili sauce

⅓   cup cider vinegar

2   tablespoons brown sugar

2   tablespoons light (mild) molasses

2   teaspoons dry mustard

1   tablespoon cornstarch

2   tablespoons water

1 In 12-inch skillet, heat oil over medium heat until hot. Add onion and cook, stirring occasionally, until tender, about 10 minutes. Add garlic and ginger and cook, stirring, 1 minute. Stir in cumin. Stir in tomatoe in puree, chili sauce, vinegar, brown sugar, molasses, and mustard; heat to boiling over high heat. Reduce heat to medium-high and cook, uncovered, 5 minutes, stirring occasionally.

2 In cup, mix cornstarch and water until blended. Stir mixture into sauce and cook until sauce boils and thickens, 1 to 2 minutes longer.

3 Cover and refrigerate, or freeze in an airtight container, if not using right away.

....

EACH ½ CUP: ABOUT 120 CALORIES, 2G PROTEIN, 25G CARBOHYDRATE, 2G TOTAL FAT (0G SATURATED), 0MG CHOLESTEROL, 655MG SODIUM

SECRET-RECIPE **Barbecue Sauce**

Pineapple adds tang to this slow-simmered sauce. Brush it over anything from hamburgers to chicken.

ACTIVE TIME: 15 MINUTES   **TOTAL TIME:** 50 MINUTES   **MAKES:** ABOUT 5 CUPS

1 tablespoon olive oil

1 large onion (12 ounces), chopped

2 tablespoons chopped, peeled fresh ginger

3 tablespoons chili powder

3 garlic cloves, crushed with garlic press

1 can (8 ounces) crushed pineapple in juice

1 can (28 ounces) crushed tomatoes in puree

⅓ cup ketchup

¼ cup cider vinegar

3 tablespoons dark brown sugar

3 tablespoons light (mild) molasses

2 teaspoons dry mustard

1 teaspoon salt

1 In 5- to 6-quart saucepot, heat oil over medium heat until hot. (Do not use a smaller pan; sauce bubbles up and splatters during cooking—the deeper the pan, the better.) Add onion and ginger; cook until onion is tender and golden, about 10 minutes, stirring occasionally. Add chili powder; cook, stirring, 1 minute. Add garlic and pineapple with its juice and cook 1 minute longer.

2 Remove pot from heat. Stir in tomatoes with their puree, ketchup, vinegar, brown sugar, molasses, mustard, and salt. Spoon one-fourth of sauce into blender. At low speed, puree until smooth. Pour sauce into bowl; repeat with remaining sauce.

3 Return sauce to saucepot; heat to boiling over high heat. Reduce heat to medium-low and cook, partially covered, stirring occasionally, until reduced to about 5 cups, about 25 minutes.

4 Cover and refrigerate if not using right away. Sauce will keep up to 1 week in refrigerator or up to 2 months in freezer.

EACH CUP: ABOUT 220 CALORIES, 3G PROTEIN, 47G CARBOHYDRATE, 3G TOTAL FAT (0G SATURATED), 0MG CHOLESTEROL, 960MG SODIUM

Salt-Free Herb RUB

Our crush of dried herbs may earn your salt shaker a well-deserved summer vacation. Use two teaspoons per pound of uncooked beef or pork, one teaspoon per pound of uncooked fish or chicken.

TOTAL TIME: 5 MINUTES   **MAKES:** ABOUT ½ CUP

- 2 tablespoons dried rosemary
- 2 tablespoons dried thyme
- 1 tablespoon dried tarragon
- 1 tablespoon coarsely ground black pepper

In mortar with pestle, or with your fingers, crush together rosemary, thyme, tarragon, and pepper. Store in airtight container and use within 6 months.

EACH TEASPOON: ABOUT 5 CALORIES, 0G PROTEIN, 1G CARBOHYDRATE, 0G TOTAL FAT (0G SATURATED), 0MG CHOLESTEROL, 1MG SODIUM

Spicy Peppercorn RUB

Our simple salt-free blend works well for steak, pork, chicken, or lamb. We like to pat about two tablespoons on a one- to two-pound steak—you can use more or less, depending on the meat's thickness.

TOTAL TIME: 10 MINUTES   **MAKES:** ABOUT ½ CUP

- 3 tablespoons coriander seeds
- 3 tablespoons cumin seeds
- 3 tablespoons fennel seeds
- 1 tablespoon whole black peppercorns

Spoon coriander seeds, cumin seeds, fennel seeds, and peppercorns into ziptight plastic bag. Place kitchen towel over bag and, with meat mallet or rolling pin, coarsely crush spices. Rub desired amount all over steak before grilling. Store in airtight container and use within 2 months.

EACH TABLESPOON: ABOUT 25 CALORIES, 2G PROTEIN, 4G CARBOHYDRATE, 1G TOTAL FAT (0G SATURATED), 0MG CHOLESTEROL, 7MG SODIUM

Cajun RUB

This spicy mix gives the protein of your choice a yummy crust. Use one tablespoon per pound of uncooked beef or pork, two teaspoons per pound of uncooked fish or chicken.

TOTAL TIME: 5 MINUTES   **MAKES:** ABOUT ⅓ CUP

2   tablespoons paprika

1   tablespoon coarsely ground black pepper

1   tablespoon ground cumin

1   tablespoon brown sugar

1   tablespoon salt

2   teaspoons ground coriander

1   teaspoon dried thyme

1   teaspoon ground red pepper (cayenne)

½   teaspoon garlic powder

½   teaspoon ground allspice

In small bowl, mix paprika, black pepper, cumin, brown sugar, salt, coriander, thyme, cayenne pepper, garlic powder, and allspice. Store in airtight container and use within 6 months.

EACH TABLESPOON: ABOUT 25 CALORIES, 1G PROTEIN, 5G CARBOHYDRATE, 1G TOTAL FAT (0G SATURATED), 0MG CHOLESTEROL, 1,400MG SODIUM

LIME-HERB **Rub**

This is wonderful rubbed under the skin of a chicken, over a pork tenderloin, or on salmon or other oily fish.

TOTAL TIME: 15 MINUTES   MAKES: ABOUT 1 CUP

2   limes

2   cups loosely packed fresh cilantro leaves, chopped

2   cups loosely packed fresh mint leaves, chopped

2   tablespoons brown sugar

2   tablespoons minced, peeled fresh ginger

3   garlic cloves, crushed with garlic press

2   green onions, thinly sliced

2   teaspoons salt

1   teaspoon crushed red pepper

1 From limes, grate 1 tablespoon peel and squeeze 2 tablespoons juice.

2 In medium bowl, combine lime peel and juice, cilantro, mint, brown sugar, ginger, garlic, green onions, salt, and crushed red pepper. Use rub right away.

EACH ¼CUP: ABOUT 70 CALORIES, 3G PROTEIN, 16G CARBOHYDRATE, 1G TOTAL FAT (0G SATURATED), 0MG CHOLESTEROL, 1,195MG SODIUM

HOISIN AND FIVE-SPICE **Glaze**

Brush this on beef, pork, chicken, or salmon during the last five minutes of grilling.

ACTIVE TIME: 1 MINUTE   TOTAL TIME: 2 MINUTES   MAKES: ABOUT 6 TABLESPOONS

¼ cup hoisin sauce

2   tablespoons soy sauce

1   teaspoon Chinese five-spice powder

In microwave-safe small bowl, stir hoisin, soy sauce, and five-spice powder. Cook, uncovered, in microwave oven on High 30 seconds, stirring once.

EACH TABLESPOON: ABOUT 30 CALORIES, 1G PROTEIN, 5G CARBOHYDRATE, 0G TOTAL FAT (0G SATURATED), 0MG CHOLESTEROL, 473MG SODIUM

SOY **Marinade**

This wonderful combination of Asian flavors turns chicken or pork into a scrumptious supper with no muss, no fuss. Simply let the meat marinate at least one hour and as long as four hours, then grill.

TOTAL TIME: 10 MINUTES   **MAKES:** ABOUT ⅔ CUP

- ⅓ **cup soy sauce**
- 3 **tablespoons seasoned rice vinegar**
- 2 **tablespoons packed brown sugar**
- 2 **tablespoons minced, peeled fresh ginger**
- 1 **tablespoon vegetable oil**
- 2 **garlic cloves, crushed with garlic press**
- 2 **green onions, thinly sliced**
- ½ **teaspoon Asian sesame oil**
- ¼ **teaspoon crushed red pepper**

In medium bowl, stir together soy sauce, vinegar, brown sugar, ginger, oil, garlic, green onions, sesame oil, and crushed red pepper.

EACH TABLESPOON: ABOUT 30 CALORIES, 1G PROTEIN, 4G CARBOHYDRATE, 1G TOTAL FAT (0G SATURATED), 0MG CHOLESTEROL, 530MG SODIUM ⊘

HONEY-MUSTARD **Glaze**

Try this on salmon, pork, or chicken.

ACTIVE TIME: 1 MINUTE   **TOTAL TIME:** 2 MINUTES   **MAKES:** ABOUT ¼ CUP

- 2 **tablespoons Dijon mustard with seeds**
- 2 **tablespoons honey**
- ½ **teaspoon dried thyme or 2 teaspoons minced fresh thyme**

In microwave-safe small bowl, stir mustard, honey, and thyme until blended. Cook, uncovered, in microwave oven on High 30 seconds, stirring once.

EACH TABLESPOON: ABOUT 40 CALORIES, 0G PROTEIN, 10G CARBOHYDRATE, 0G TOTAL FAT (0G SATURATED), 0MG CHOLESTEROL, 180MG SODIUM ⊘

Index

Note: Page numbers in *italics* indicate photos.

Photography Credits

Antonio Achilleos: 12, 54, 72

James Baigrie: 20, 27, 34, 67, 77, 103

Courtesy of Sears: 8

Tara Donne: 110

Getty Images: Annabelle Breakey. 105

Brian Hagiwara: 25, 48, 53, 64, 80, 85, 107

Lisa Hubbard: 6

iStockPhoto: 114; Mark Gillow, 15; Oliver Hoffmann, 109 (zucchini); Hudiemm, 46

Rita Maas: 17

Kate Mathis: 63, 88, 101, 115

Off Set: Con Poulos, 2

Alan Richardson: 28, 31, 41, 70, 93, 96

Shutterstock: Denio109, 108; Fortish, 69; Elena Moiseeva, 121; Smit, 78; TAGSTOCK1, 109 (broccoli)

Studio D: Jesus Ayala, 118; Philip Friedman, 7, 22, 37, 82, 117; Lara Robby, 61

FRONT COVER: Con Poulos/Off Set
BACK COVER: Kate Mathis

Metric Conversion Charts

The recipes that appear in this cookbook use the standard United States method for measuring liquid and dry or solid ingredients (teaspoons, tablespoons, and cups). The information on this chart is provided to help cooks outside the U.S. successfully use these recipes. All equivalents are approximate.

METRIC EQUIVALENTS FOR DIFFERENT TYPES OF INGREDIENTS

STANDARD CUP (e.g. flour)	FINE POWDER (e.g. sugar)	GRAIN (e.g. rice)	GRANULAR (e.g. butter)	LIQUID SOLIDS (e.g. milk)	LIQUID
¾	105 g	113 g	143 g	150 g	180 ml
⅔	93 g	100 g	125 g	133 g	160 ml
½	70 g	75 g	95 g	100 g	120 ml
⅓	47 g	50 g	63 g	67 g	80 ml
¼	35 g	38 g	48 g	50 g	60 ml
⅛	18 g	19 g	24 g	25 g	30 ml

USEFUL EQUIVALENTS FOR LIQUID INGREDIENTS BY VOLUME

¼ tsp	=						1 ml
½ tsp	=						2 ml
1 tsp	=						5 ml
3 tsp	=	1 tbls	=		½ fl oz	=	15 ml
		2 tbls	=	⅛ cup	=	1 fl oz	=	30 ml
		4 tbls	=	¼ cup	=	2 fl oz	=	60 ml
		5⅓ tbls	=	⅓ cup	=	3 fl oz	=	80 ml
		8 tbls	=	½ cup	=	4 fl oz	=	120 ml
		10⅔ tbls	=	⅔ cup	=	5 fl oz	=	160 ml
		12 tbls	=	¾ cup	=	6 fl oz	=	180 ml
		16 tbls	=	1 cup	=	8 fl oz	=	240 ml
		1 pt	=	2 cups	=	16 fl oz	=	480 ml
		1 qt	=	4 cups	=	32 fl oz	=	960 ml
						33 fl oz	=	1000 ml = 1 L

USEFUL EQUIVALENTS FOR DRY INGREDIENTS BY WEIGHT
(To convert ounces to grams, multiply the number of ounces by 30.)

1 oz	=	¹⁄₁₆ lb	=	30 g
2 oz	=	¼ lb	=	120 g
4 oz	=	½ lb	=	240 g
8 oz	=	¾ lb	=	360 g
16 oz	=	1 lb	=	480 g

USEFUL EQUIVALENTS FOR COOKING/OVEN TEMPERATURES

	Fahrenheit	Celsius	Gas Mark
Freeze Water	32° F	0° C	
Room Temperature	68° F	20° C	
Boil Water	212° F	100° C	
Bake	325° F	160° C	3
	350° F	180° C	4
	375° F	190° C	5
	400° F	200° C	6
	425° F	220° C	7
	450° F	230° C	8
Broil			Grill

USEFUL EQUIVALENTS LENGTH
(To convert inches to centimeters, multiply the number of inches by 2.5.)

1 in	=			2.5 cm	
6 in	=	½ ft	=	15 cm	
12 in	=	1 ft	=	30 cm	
36 in	=	3 ft	= 1 yd	=	90 cm
40 in	=			100 cm	= 1 m